CREATING CAIN

CREATING CAIN

MY FATHER'S
SURPRISING STORY
OF LOVE, SUCCESS,
DECEIT, AND LOSS

J. P. Hays

LUMINARE PRESS
WWW.LUMINAREPRESS.COM

CREATING CAIN
My Father's Surprising Story of Love, Success, Deceit, and Loss

Copyright © 2024 by J.P. Hays

All rights reserved. This book or any portion thereof may not be reproduced or used in any manner whatsoever without the express written permission of the publisher, except for the use of brief quotations in a book review.

Printed in the United States of America

Luminare Press
442 Charnelton St.
Eugene, OR 97401
www.luminarepress.com

LCCN: 2024915328
ISBN: 979-8-88679-646-9

Dedications

In loving memory of my parents, Wilmer and Carol Hays, whose love, generosity, and inspiration fueled not only this story, but my entire life.

For my sister, Sara, who is the only other person who knows firsthand what it was like to be loved and raised by these incredible people. I love you and appreciate your constant support and encouragement in every facet of my life.

For my beloved wife, Beth Ann, there aren't enough words to describe how much you mean to me and the level of love that I feel for you. You are my best friend and partner, and I am so fortunate that I can walk life's trails and experience "new roads" with you. I appreciate your love, support, and encouragement every day. You are my forever!

And for my children Taylor Ann and Kevin. There isn't enough room on this page to describe the depth of love I have for you two. You are the lights of my life, and my heart overflows each day with joy and pride for the children you were and the adults you have become.

Introduction

Most children who were born into or lived through the late 1920s and early 1930s saw firsthand how the Great Depression affected their families and the many hardships created by the daily grind of struggle. To this generation, achieving success became more than just a dream, it truly was a requirement.

To them, it simply was not enough to provide their families with just a little more than their parents did them. They knew that money was the key to happiness and security, and this generation would do anything they could to make it.

My father was Wilmer Hays. He was one of those children and no different than most. His family struggled throughout his young life, and while he often dreamed of success and having money, there was no clear-cut way for him to make a better life for himself. He would not have any opportunity for an education outside of what he learned on the farm or in small, rural schoolhouses. His reality was that he thought he was nothing more than a farmhand whose only purpose was to complete the work his father didn't have time to do or that his brother thought he was too good to do. It was a difficult position to be in, wanting to have a better life but not having any real chance to make it happen.

My dad as a child had very few memories of playing with friends or spending any time with his father that wasn't related to work on the farm. In stark contrast to that,

I learned very early on in my childhood that Dad's experiences and upbringing were very different than my own. I grew up with fond memories of almost every aspect of my childhood and along with that, felt a strong sense of being loved and protected by my dad. While I was fortunate to feel the security and joy of having a father who loved me, he also made it clear to me that he was invested in both teaching me and leading me by example.

His patience, encouragement, and life lessons helped shape who I am today. And as I reflect now on my early years, I realize that although I always felt loved by my dad, there was always a line that separated us. For me, it was always something just below the surface that as an adolescent, and then later as a teenager, was much more difficult for me to understand. But as I grew older, that perceived rift between us became easier to identify and ultimately comprehend. What I viewed as a divide was just that he was the father, and I was the son. And the disconnect that I discerned in my youth was just that my dad and I were never equals or peers, and certainly not friends. He was the teacher, and I was the student. And I am not confessing any of this now as any slight to my dad because the truth of the matter is that I have loved him every day of my life, and he was everything to me.

Several years before his death, Dad confided to my sister that he thought I was his hero. It may seem odd for me to say this, but when my sister shared that with me, it was very difficult for me to hear. Don't get me wrong, I was touched by him saying that, and even more so, that he felt that way about me.

But as I think back on all the great things he said to me, all the encouragement he gave, and the patience and positive reinforcement he provided, calling me his hero may have been the thing I appreciated most. But for as much as I tried to do for him, and as hard as I worked to make him proud of me, the hard truth of the matter is that he was mine.

As I search through my memory now, it is hard for me to pinpoint the precise moment that Dad and I started to grow closer and arrived at the point where he would be self-assured and comfortable enough to say that about me. But I suspect it was when I started to have more in common with him as an adult, husband, and father in my own right. When I began to demonstrate, with some level of proficiency, all the things he spent a lifetime teaching me. Lessons of love, character, kindness, and responsibility. It may have been when I got married or had children of my own. Or when I purchased my first house or finally provided some stability for my family by landing a good job that included benefits. All those things were important to Dad and became evidence that the time he spent teaching me was not wasted.

The typical things that most children do as they become adults and start displaying abilities to stand on their own two feet. That allow children to begin dismantling the safety nets their parents spent a lifetime providing them. So, when I purchased my first house, I chose to live just two blocks from my parents so our family could see each other frequently and my kids would have constant contact with their grandparents.

With a family of my own now, I watched from a close distance as my parents aged and their health declined. And when their needs for added attention and care increased, I would stop in to visit with them each day.

I was busy with my own life, but I knew the time we spent together was important to me and was equally if not more so to them. Once the pleasantries of small talk, the weather, or whatever new aches and pains were bothering them were done, we would typically spend more and more time just talking about the past. It was a way to distract them from the present and the fragility of aging, and I would enjoy seeing Dad's face light up as he remembered fondly the times he spent with Mom as teenagers and then as newlyweds. But I also remember seeing the pain on his face as he told stories that described how difficult life was for him as a child, how hard he worked on the family farm, and how badly he wanted love and approval from his father. He would tell me how much his father struggled in his life and that from his young perspective, he thought that money could or would have solved so many of his dad's problems. So, from a very early age, it was important to Dad that he achieve some level of success in his life, and as a young man, he equated success with accumulating money.

Dad's mind was clear, and his memory still good, but he insisted on repeating one of his earliest childhood memories that occurred when he was just six years old.

He told me that one night he was awakened by yelling coming from the kitchen downstairs. He said he looked over at his older brother's bed, but that the shouting did not wake him up. So, he decided to climb out of bed and snuck down the stairs alone. Quietly tiptoeing through the dark dining room, he used the cover of darkness to silently crawl between the chairs to get under the dining room table where he would have a clear view of what was happening. He knew that he could not be discovered, or he would "get the belt."

That was something he feared about his father, and that reality stayed with him throughout his adolescence.

From his vantage point he saw his mother sitting at the kitchen table, her face illuminated brightly by the light fixture hanging from the ceiling in front of her. As she looked up at his father, Dad saw that her face was flush, and a steady stream of tears ran down her cheeks. Each time I heard this story, Dad would describe the look on his mother's face as one of "pain and disappointment."

He remembered seeing a man he did not recognize moving toward the kitchen door, and as he grabbed the knob to pull the door open, the man looked back at his father and with a cold look said, "Ralph, we've known each other a long time, and I helped you out when you needed a place, but at the end of the day, you are just a tenant farmer here. I know that times are tough, they're tough on all of us, but if you can't pay the rent, then I need to get someone in here that can. I'm sorry, Ralph, but I need you and Lucille out by the end of the month."

As the door closed, Dad watched quietly and tried his best to stay still as his mother sobbed and cried out, "What are we going to do? Every year or two, it's start over, work harder, and do more with less. We don't have any money, and now we don't have anywhere to go. We've got four kids sleeping upstairs. What are we going to do?"

Dad was smart and knew even at six years of age that he and his family would be moving again. This would mean a new address, a new school, and new classmates, but more of the same difficult life, just with different scenery. This trend would follow him throughout his young life, and he realized in that moment that having money was the key to having a better life.

That was the first of many family moves that Dad remembered before he skipped ahead about ten years and reminded me of his family's last move to LaSalle in the fall of 1949. Once again, a story I had heard many times before because that was the year he met my mother. He told me the story of how they met on his first day of school and how much time they spent together. And then about the first time he walked Mom home from school. Mom's parents had money, so she lived in the most expensive and exclusive part of town. Dad said that he had never seen houses like these before, and from the moment they turned the corner onto Mom's street, he looked at each house and couldn't even imagine what it would be like to live in such a place.

Dad often shared with me that he felt like his father didn't think he was good enough, and I knew how hard that was for him to deal with growing up. But as he reflected on that day walking up to Mom's house with her for the first time, he remembered that it was the very first time that he consciously doubted himself and felt like maybe his father was right, maybe he wasn't good enough. Maybe not only to be there with this incredible girl but also to even step inside one of these beautiful homes.

But Dad looked over to me and smiled as he said, "But your mother didn't allow that feeling to last very long as she told me, 'Someday you will buy me a house like this.' Mom gave me confidence and let me know every day that she believed in me, and it was the very first time in my life that I had someone like that. Someone who really saw me for who I was, supported and encouraged me, and was genuinely interested in knowing, and partnering, with me. And she knew that I believed in her too, so it did not take us long to decide that we would work together to build the life we dreamed of."

Dad continued, "Everything changed for me after I met your mom. And everything was going great…but little did I know then that my life was going to change so dramatically because of a man I'd never met." When Dad said that my ears perked up and my interest focused because I was sure that I had never heard this part of the story before. A man I'd never met? That was definitely something new and that I needed to hear more about, so I leaned forward in my seat and listened closely as Dad said, "I had never even heard his name before. But now it's a name I'll never forget. That man's name was Sam Livingston."

CHAPTER 1

The Beginning

1956

An illuminated clock on the bank at the end of the block showed it was just before 11 p.m. on what had turned out to be a very busy election night. Officials from the 12th precinct election headquarters had been busy tallying ballots from precincts throughout the city and surrounding suburbs since the polls closed at 7 p.m. On that cool November night, the streets of Chicago were quiet as a lone yellow Checker cab sat idling along the curb outside election headquarters. Steam was slowly rising from the heat of its exhaust pipe when suddenly a young woman pushed open the heavy, glass front door and rushed outside. With her overcoat unbuttoned, she wore a white blouse under a navy blue blazer and a matching short skirt. Her black, high-heeled pumps clacked loudly on the concrete sidewalk as she ran toward the cab. She opened the rear door, slid into the back seat, and told the cabbie, "Thanks for waiting. Let's go back to the Belmont as fast as you can."

Just a few minutes later, the cab screeched to an abrupt stop under the Belmont Hotel canopy. The woman shoved a small wad of cash at the driver and bolted from the cab, brushing past the doorman and into the hotel. Her shoes clacked loudly as she ran on the polished marble floor of the hotel lobby and headed toward the elevators. She stepped into the lift and reached out to hit the button for the fourth floor. While the carriage climbed upward, she straightened a small white campaign pin on her lapel that had "LIVINGSTON" spelled out in red letters with bright blue outlines. The elevator doors opened, and she ran down the hallway, her shoes now silenced by the plush carpeting, and arrived at suite 411 where another "LIVINGSTON" campaign sign was taped to the door.

    A small group of Livingston's inner circle, which included campaign managers, other campaign staffers like her, and several large-money donors, were scattered throughout the smoke-filled hospitality suite. They milled around high-top tables set with white linens, candles, and fresh-cut flower centerpieces as servers circled the room with cocktails and hors d'oeuvres on large silver platters. The crowd was talking, laughing, and mingling, but their eyes paid close attention to television sets positioned around the room, broadcasting live election results. At the bar against the far wall of the room, several men smoked cigars, sipped neat single malt, and laughed in their own smaller clique. The woman scanned the room, found the man she was looking for, and made her way through the crowd to where he stood with his back to her. She placed her left hand on his right shoulder, raised herself on her toes, and whispered in his ear, "The count is in; they should make the call soon."

    Minutes later, a telephone rang, and a man yelled out, "Quiet! This is it!" The man answered the phone, "Hello…. Yes, he's right here." He turned with the phone, extended the handset, and said, "Sam, it's him." Livingston took the phone and said, "Hello, Tom." The room fell silent as they could only hear one side of the conversation. They watched Livingston closely and tried to get some clues to what was being said, but he stood emotionless as he listened. Then a big smile began to emerge on his face as he raised his left fist in the air and said, "I appreciate that, Tom, thank you very much. We are going to work as hard as we can for the people of Cook County." Livingston hung up the phone, and the room erupted as Livingston addressed the crowd, "Fourteen months ago, we decided that Cook County needed change. We ran on a platform of youth, energy, and the need to get back to law and order. And because of all your dedication, hard work, and support, we won. Waller just conceded. Let's make the announcement."

Livingston grabbed his suit coat and put it on as the entire group filed out of the hotel suite in celebration. Livingston was tall, thin, athletic, and made long, graceful strides as he walked confidently down the long hallway. He was a handsome man with full, wavy, light-brown hair kept trimmed short and neatly combed with a part on the side. He was clean-shaven and professional in his grooming and typically wore a tailored three-piece suit that included his newly adopted, trademark monochromatic plaid vest; it all fit him flawlessly. He paired that with light-colored shoes that highlighted his sense of style.

As the group made the walk down the long hallway toward the grand ballroom, the muffled roar of an even larger gathering began to fill the hallway. The ballroom doors swung open, and the noise and energy from inside the room were palpable, washing over everyone in its path. From that doorway, the stage seemed a mile away, and hanging over the stage was a huge banner with a field of white, with "LIVINGSTON" spelled out in large red letters with blue outlines.

The banner was every bit of twenty feet high but fit perfectly with the scale of the grand ballroom. A man was speaking at the podium at the opposite end of the room, but he was not clearly visible through the light haze of cigar and cigarette smoke, which was continually highlighted by the motion of bright spotlights trying to find their way through to the stage. He finally noticed Livingston's campaign manager signaling him with a flashlight as he squinted against the bright lights and saw Livingston standing in the doorway. He pointed his finger to direct the crowd's attention and said, "Now please welcome our next Cook County state's attorney, Samuel Livingston!"

As Livingston started his long walk to the stage, red, white, and blue confetti fell from the ceiling to the eagerly awaiting crowd below as hundreds of red and blue balloons were also released. The crowd below swatted balloons around the room like beach balls in celebration as Livingston raised his arms to wave to the crowd while smiling and making eye contact with those standing closest to the aisle. Livingston had the look of an up-and-coming political figure, and at only thirty-eight years old, he was the youngest man ever elected to this position. As he reached the podium, the crowd fell silent in anticipation.

Livingston started with an emphatic "We did it!" as he raised both arms above his head. The crowd roared back in applause and cheers. Livingston had a flair for the dramatic and knew how to work a room, so he waited patiently before he continued, "But more importantly, we did it together!" This time he emphasized the word "together." Livingston spoke on with a softer and more deliberate tone. "I just got a call from our current state attorney and our opponent in this campaign, Tom Waller." A small spattering of boos came from the crowd as he raised his hands again to quiet that reaction. "Tom was very gracious on the phone and has conceded this election. I commended him on his efforts. I think we both ran clean campaigns, and I think that we both care about this city and this county. I made a commitment to all of you who live and work in Cook County that we will no longer go along with the status quo."

The crowd cheered back in unison. "LIV-ING-STON, LIV-ING-STON, LIV-ING-STON." Livingston beamed acceptance and confidence as he said, "We are taking back our streets!"

He slammed his hand down emphatically on the podium as he said, "We are taking back our neighborhoods!"

Then again as he said, "We are taking back our businesses!"

To overcome the noise from the crowd, he yelled into the microphone, "And we are getting back to law and order!" That drew the loudest response of all.

Livingston again put his hands up to calm the crowd to listen, then softened his tone again to draw the room in. "Our message is this. If you pay your taxes, you should be able to walk safely down your street, day or night. You should be able to send your kids off to school without fearing for their safety." Livingston started to add some volume and brought it to a crescendo, saying, "And if you work hard and invest sixteen hours a day owning and operating a small or family business, you should not have to be shaken down by the mob every month. Or be threatened or intimidated until you do pay.

"So, here is my message to all the criminals in our city. You should expect to be caught, prosecuted, and jailed. If you are going to do the crime, you are going to do the time!

"And to all of you who are either in the mob or working for the mob, you should expect some sleepless nights ahead.

Because we are coming for you. All of you! We are no longer going to allow you to control our lives, extort money from our businesses, and treat us like outsiders in our own city." The crowd roared with applause before Livingston concluded with, "My promise to all of you is this. We will take back our city, our streets, and our neighborhoods.

"And that work starts tonight!"

THE DRAKE HOTEL, SUITE 1310, THE PENTHOUSE SUITE and the most plush, exclusive, and alluring room in Chicago. The lakefront location provided beautiful views of Lake Michigan and the surrounding high-rise buildings. With floor-to-ceiling windows, it also provided spectacular nighttime views of the city lights below. Soft piano music played from the console along the far wall while room service had provided a small bistro table for two set up next to the windows. Empty plates were the last remnants of a completed romantic dinner for two. The only light in the room came from candles on the table, which had burned so far down that wax covered the brass holders and had begun to drip onto the white linen tablecloth below. With empty champaign bottles turned upside down in ice buckets, one empty champaign flute had a pronounced mark of bright red lipstick on its rim.

A trail of abandoned clothing led to the bedroom door where a statuesque blonde swung the door open slowly, wearing only her sheer, black lace corselet. Candlelight reflected perfectly off her beautiful face and smooth skin as she moved quietly, gathering her clothing off the floor. She paused briefly at the table and gently blew out the candles before walking quietly with her clothes in hand to the living room sofa. She sat and slipped on her stockings, then her tight-fitting, red strapless dress before leaning forward to slide on her red high-heel pumps. Once dressed, she walked to the hall closet and retrieved her overcoat, which she simply draped over her shoulders and left the room. She walked confidently down the long hallway toward the elevators, not seeming to care who might see her there. She pushed the down button and took notice of herself in the reflection of the elevator doors.

She reached into her purse to retrieve her red lipstick and used the mirror finish of the brass doors to touch up her lips as she waited.

Meanwhile, two well-dressed men in overcoats walked into the hotel lobby on a cold, windy, and late December night. Livingston, one of those two men, removed his gloves and blew warm air onto his hands. The other man entered behind Livingston and took one last drag from his cigarette before extinguishing it in the ashtray just inside the door. Both men wore Fedoras and long dark overcoats as they walked together to the registration desk. The night clerk made eye contact with Livingston and nodded at him as Livingston walked directly to the counter and slid a $20 bill across the polished marble countertop. The clerk exchanged the money for a room key with 1310 stamped on the tag. Livingston took the key and walked directly to the elevators. As the bell chimed, the doors opened, and the beautiful well-dressed blonde exited the elevator. Livingston kept his head down while his colleague politely tipped his hat and smiled as they passed.

Both men entered the vacated elevator car, and as the doors closed, Livingston hit the button for the thirteenth floor as his colleague asked in a gravelly voice, "Boss, did you see who that was?"

Livingston answered, "Yes, Franklin, that's why we're here."

Franklin inquired, "So we're going after Lennox and the Outfit?"

Livingston answered right back, "That we are!"

The doors opened on the thirteenth floor, and Livingston and Franklin made their way down that very same hallway. Franklin, still wearing his hat, overcoat, and gloves, appeared a bit winded as he struggled to keep up with the long effortless strides of Livingston. Franklin was shorter, stockier, and appeared to be several years older than Livingston.

He had a tougher persona and far more weathered face, which was growing increasingly flushed from the walk and the heat trapped by his heavy coat and hat. They stood quietly in front of the door to Suite 1310 as Livingston whispered, "You ready?"

Franklin nodded and took a deep breath as Livingston slowly slid the key into the door and pushed it open silently. With the curtains open, the only light in the room came from the neighboring buildings. So, they carefully made their way through the suite and into the bedroom, where they stood quietly over the man sleeping in the bed.

Franklin, who still had his gloves on, placed his hand securely over the mouth of the man sleeping and pushed down firmly to keep him from moving or making any noise. Livingston turned on the light from the nightstand and leaned over the man until just a few inches from his face. The man in the bed was wide awake now, his eyes wide open. Livingston could see the uncertainty and fear in his eyes as he spoke softly but with a deliberate and somewhat menacing tone, "Do you know who I am?" The man nodded under the continued pressure of being restrained. Livingston grinned and said, "Good."

Livingston was an experienced lawyer and enjoyed creating drama in these kinds of situations, so he made each of these statements short to build suspense in Garrett's mind, "And I know who you are. You are Thomas Garrett. You are the president of City Bank of Chicago and the youngest bank president in the entire city. You live in Oak Park in a very big and I'm guessing very expensive house. It's a nice neighborhood, very exclusive. And I know that you have a beautiful wife at home named Janice that you married just three years ago." Livingston took a longer pause. "You know what else I know?

I know that was Catherine Lennox that just left this room."

As Garrett heard that, the fear and uncertainty in his eyes changed to panic and surrender as he faced the realization that he had been caught and that Lennox would kill him if he ever found out he was sleeping with his wife. Livingston continued, "So, I have just two questions for you, Mr. Garrett. And I need your answers right fucking now. Am I going to talk to Aiden Lennox?" Garrett shook his head emphatically no. "Or am I going to talk to you?" Garrett nodded in a resigned acceptance. "Now my colleague here is going to remove his hand, and we are going to sit together and talk. Do you understand?" Garrett nodded and Franklin released his grip from Garrett's mouth.

Garrett sat up in bed shirtless, and his smooth muscular chest showed his young, athletic physique. He had a full head of thick, wavy blond hair, steely blue eyes, and a chiseled strong chin that made it easy to see why Catherine Lennox was so attracted to him. Garrett was everything her husband was not. He was young, in remarkably good shape, beautiful to look at, and an enthusiastic lover. And perhaps what she enjoyed the most was that he allowed her to be in control. That was something her husband never allowed.

Garrett took a few deep breaths and tried to compose himself as Livingston looked back at him from the bedroom doorway and said with a great deal of satisfaction, "You work for me now. Don't keep me waiting."

CHAPTER 2

The Raid

1957

It was just before noon on a sunny but unseasonably cool April morning as a caravan of black sedans traveled through busy Chicago streets. The sidewalks were crowded with pedestrians and shoppers, most of whom were bundled in warm coats and hats while others walked swiftly with their hands in their pockets as they made the quick trip outside on their lunch break. They all contributed to the hustle and bustle as the six cars weaved through the city.

The cars came to a single-file-stop at the Washington Street drawbridge, which was raised to allow a large barge to pass along the Chicago River below. Once the barge cleared, the bridge tender lowered the bridge, the flashing red stoplights changed back to green, and the caravan continued across Washington Street. The tires hummed as they crossed the steel bridge grates before the street surface changed back to smooth asphalt. After another few blocks, they made the right turn onto LaSalle Street and pulled up along the curb in front of City Bank of Chicago.

Men dressed in black suits exited their cars and rushed toward the front door of the bank. As they pushed through the heavy glass door, the first man in held up a gold badge with "FBI" on it for all to see in his left hand as his right hand rested gently on the .38 revolver strapped to his hip. He announced, "FBI... Don't anyone move." The remaining agents rushed past him as customers and staff alike were startled and screamed in fear as they dropped to the floor.

That morning the typically quiet bank lobby was noisy and chaotic from the earlier breach.

Meanwhile, Thomas Garret sat in his office toward the back of the bank, and throughout all the noise and activity from the lobby, he sat motionless with his elbows on his desk holding his head in his hands. He did not appear surprised or even bothered by the commotion and seemed to know exactly what was happening and even expected it.

A young male teller led two agents down the long hallway and knocked on the closed office door just below the engraved nameplate that read "Thomas Garrett—President." The teller announced loudly through the closed door, "Mr. Garrett, the FBI are here to see you, sir."

THE FOLLOWING MORNING, THE SUN HAD JUST BEGUN TO rise over Lake Michigan in the affluent suburb of Evanston, located just north of the Chicago city limits. Cold overnight temperatures had caused the large, red-brick home to be enveloped by the fog gently rolling in from the warm water of Lake Michigan. The morning silence in the large, second-floor bedroom was interrupted by soft music and water running from the adjacent bathroom.

A man wearing boxer shorts, a white undershirt, and black socks stood alone at the sink as he shaved for work. He too was enveloped in steam as he wiped away the condensation from the mirror in front of him. While music played softly on a radio next to him, he rested his left hand on the sink and leaned in to shave with his right. With hot water running into the sink, he wiped condensation from the mirror periodically to see what he was doing.

He was a man in his fifties, still in good shape but had added some plump with age. While he stood at the sink, his profile showed a bit of a belly, but his arms and shoulders were still muscular and well-defined although quite hairy. His dark hair, kept short and neatly trimmed, was predominantly gray just around the temples. His face was handsome with dark full eyebrows, a full mustache, and dark eyes that seemed to have an intentional squint. He also had a strong, defined jawline with rough and weathered skin that added to his strong and rugged good looks.

As the music ended, the radio announcer updated the morning news, "This morning the FBI is sharing more details about the raid on a downtown bank yesterday. The new Cook County state's attorney, Samuel Livingston, who campaigned in the last election for tougher enforcement and for prosecution of mob activity here in Chicago, appears to have started to deliver on those promises. An FBI source close to the investigation was quoted this morning saying nearly 8 million dollars of mob money was seized during the raid yesterday."

When he heard that, he pounded his hand down hard on the sink, causing water to splash everywhere and his shaving cup and brush to be knocked into the sink. He turned the radio off and reached for the neatly folded towel next to the sink. He wiped the water from the porcelain sink top and then the remaining shaving cream from his cheeks and neck. He looked in the mirror and saw his anger staring back. He also saw frustration and a plan for whoever it was who had betrayed him. Then he noticed a single hair out of place in his perfectly trimmed mustache and reached down for the scissors to trim it. He looked back at himself in the mirror and now seemed pleased with what he saw. And just like that, he had turned the switch from anger back to vanity.

He opened the bathroom door and walked into the spacious bedroom adorned with expensive antiquities and ornate Victorian furniture. A portrait of him and his wife was hung above the fireplace mantle in a large gold frame. In the painting, he stood proudly behind his wife wearing a black tuxedo, black studs, and a black crossover tie while she was seated in a plush, black velvet chair in front of him, wearing a now-familiar, sexy, red strapless evening dress. She sat with her shapely long legs crossed, which were accentuated by her high hemline and red high-heel pumps. They made a very attractive couple.

He pushed the sliding doors of his closet open and selected a plain, white dress shirt from a row of nearly forty other pressed and neatly arranged shirts on hangers. He slid his arms into each shirt sleeve as he moved to his right and selected a gray pinstripe suit from an assortment of a couple of dozen other suits all arranged by color. He walked over and laid the suit flat on the bed. All the while, his wife was asleep across from him.

He sat on the bench at the foot of the bed to put on his trousers before he walked back over to the closet to select a belt and a pair of shoes. His left hand slid across his many belts like wind chimes as he selected one that matched the black wingtip shoes that he grabbed from the shelf to his right. He returned to the bench and stood quietly feeding his belt through the loops in his pants as he watched his wife sleep.

He sat to put on his shoes and then walked back to the dresser and grabbed the handles with both hands to pull open a wide drawer lined with green velvet. Inside this drawer were only cuff links and watches, and he selected a pair of gold cuff links with a beautiful pearl inlay. Then he looked over a variety of wrist and pocket watches and selected a gold pocket watch, which he flipped open to reveal that it too had a pearl face.

The time was 7:15 as he wound the crown and gently slid it into his vest pocket. He moved back to the closet and grabbed his shoulder holster off the hook. He slid the well-oiled brown leather over both arms and adjusted it to fit before he returned to pull open the lowest drawer of the dresser. This drawer contained half a dozen pistols all laid out against dark blue velvet. He selected a chrome-plated .38 caliber revolver from the drawer and slid it firmly into the holster.

He sat on the side of the bed and gently slid his cuff links through his shirt cuffs as he looked back over his shoulder at his wife sleeping. Her head rested on a large, white satin pillow that matched the satin sheets on the bed. She was a stunningly beautiful woman with long, blonde wavy hair, a thin nose, and thin, penciled eyebrows. She was clearly many years younger than him, and although she was not wearing makeup, her face was beautiful and her complexion perfect. You could spend time searching for imperfections, but you would find none. Her white silk nightgown was cut low and highlighted her ample cleavage as the thin spaghetti straps rested loosely on her shoulders and showed plenty of her smooth, young skin.

He walked toward the bedroom door and slid on his suit coat before he stopped for an extended pause to look back at his wife. And although he stood silently, his face indicated conflict and some signs of indecision. He sensed a change in his marriage and appeared to struggle with his feelings. He was a tough man and did not allow himself to be emotional; he thought it would cloud his judgment, make him appear weak, or affect his ability to react to certain requirements. He did love this woman, but his face showed some indication of betrayal. He had recognized a noticeable change in her. He grabbed the doorknob and left the bedroom without saying a word.

Floorboards creaked as he made his way down the staircase and neared the kitchen; he saw that lights were on and could hear activity from inside. As he pushed the large, swinging door open, the maid was making coffee by the stove. Ada was an older woman who had worked for Lennox for many years and was an established part of caring for the Lennoxs and their estate. She was short and heavyset with gray hair kept neatly in a tight bun on her head. She wore a plain gray house dress with white trim and collar and a full-length white apron. She had piercing light blue eyes, a soft voice, and a caring personality.

She saw Lennox more as a son than an employer but always insisted on showing her respect for him and his position by adding mister to his first name when she addressed him, "Good morning, Mr. Aiden. Would you like coffee?"

Lennox replied, "Good morning, Ada. Not this morning, I need to get on the road." He moved through the kitchen toward the table as Ada walked to him with his overcoat draped over her arm and today's newspaper in her hand. Lennox took the newspaper and slid it into his briefcase as Ada assisted him with his overcoat and said, "Have a good day, Mr. Aiden." Only offering a polite but short, "Thank you, Ada," he walked out the back door and toward the large, detached garage. It matched the house with its red-brick façade and white trim and had dark green English ivy that covered parts of the brick walls. Lennox opened the first of three garage doors to reveal a burgundy-red Chrysler Imperial Newport.

He started the car and slowly backed it out of the garage; every piece of perfectly polished chrome and paint sparkled as the bright garage lights from overhead danced over it. This car reflected its owner. It was the very best that money could buy, and Aiden Lennox would not drive anything less.

He drove along his carefully manicured gardens and lawn toward the main road where he turned right to head north on Sheridan Road toward Lake Forest. He was headed to the home of his boss and the leader of the Chicago mob called "The Outfit," Salvador La Monica.

After about thirty-five minutes, he passed a sign that read "Lake Forest, population 8,700." By that time, the sun had risen enough for him to see that the tree-lined streets had large, beautiful mansions on both sides with each one seemingly larger and grander than the last. He turned left onto a narrow one-lane road that wound through fence-lined horse pastures and stables. As he approached the main gate, he could see the silhouette of a large man standing in front of the twenty-foot-tall, wrought-iron gates. As his car moved closer, the headlights helped to illuminate the man, and Lennox saw the familiar face of Mike Baker.

Baker, a long-time member of La Monica's personal security team, was a large man and a former Golden Glove junior boxing champion who spent a short time working as a policeman. But Baker enjoyed violence a little too much and had several allegations of excessive force and brutality made against him, so his time as a policeman was short-lived. La Monica liked that Baker had an edge and a mean streak and could do whatever was asked of him. But Baker was also intelligent and articulate, and La Monica saw a lot of himself in Baker when he offered him a job.

Baker recognized the car, calmly walked to the driver's window, and said, "Good morning, Mr. Lennox."

Lennox replied, "Good morning, Mike" as Baker signaled to open the gate. The large, wrought-iron gates swung open slowly, and the Chrysler Imperial proceeded through. Most mornings there were quiet, so the only sound was that of the gravel rustling under Lennox's tires as he continued toward the main house.

The Italianate mansion of nearly thirty-thousand square feet had been built in the early 1900s by the very famous and extremely wealthy Armour family. The house was situated on about twelve hundred acres that included stables, pastures, and a formal garden designed and constructed by world-renowned landscape architect Jens Jensen. Every detail of the house was elaborate and ornate. The marble, bronze railings and wood-carved panels were all imported from Europe during the almost four years of construction in the early 1900s.

Lake Forest was home to some of the country's wealthiest businessmen and their families; this was generally referred to as "old money," and this level of wealth and privilege always seemed insulated from trouble happening elsewhere in the country. La Monica had his eye on Lake Forest for many years and wanted in.

The Armour estate was considered one of the finest in the entire country, and when the Armours lost everything in the stock market crash of 1929 and the Great Depression that followed, the property changed hands several times before La Monica purchased it at auction for a small fraction of its original ten-million-dollar price tag.

The Chrysler Imperial drove into the circular driveway at the front of the house, which had a large limestone fountain in the center and was surrounded by perfectly manicured boxwood shrubs and annual flowers. Lennox parked his car and walked to the front door, where he was greeted by the butler who said, "Good morning, Mr. Lennox" as he took his overcoat. Lennox made the familiar walk along the smooth and polished marble floor of the long corridor before making his way up the grand marble staircase. At the top of the stairs, he found the door to the office open and walked in to find La Monica sitting alone quietly at the head of the large, wooden conference table.

La Monica was a second-generation Italian American who grew up in the mob working for Al Capone, first as a driver and then as an enforcer. Now he was fifty-six years of age and had risen to the position of "Chieftain." He was calling the shots and involved in leading every aspect of Outfit business. Though short and thin, he had a commanding presence and a reputation for violence. He did not take shit from anyone. His dark hair had started to thin and turn gray, and he had developed some male-pattern baldness. He clung to the last of his thinning hair but was not overly concerned with trying to hide it. He compensated for that by being perfectly groomed and impeccably dressed. He had dark sunken eyes and was clean-shaven, and his large nose was the predominant feature on his face. That day, like most, he wore a custom-tailored suit from Italy and an imported silk tie.

La Monica sat with a stern and agitated expression as he saw Lennox enter. As La Monica's right-hand man, Lennox was responsible for all the day-to-day business and finance operations of the Outfit. And although Lennox looked like, and was, a successful businessman, he could also be ruthless and was not afraid to get his hands dirty when it came to mob business. Lennox was promoted into this position when La Monica made Chieftain, and there was no one whom La Monica trusted more.

Though Lennox was not a blood relative or even Italian, La Monica viewed him as family and treated him like a son. Lennox walked to the end of the table and greeted La Monica with a handshake and a kiss on the cheek before he placed his briefcase on the table to his right. La Monica told him, "Aiden, there is breakfast and coffee" as he pointed toward the hospitality table that his staff had set up along the far wall of the office.

Lennox walked over and filled a coffee cup; as he turned back, he found La Monica standing directly behind him and said, "Walk with me" as he pushed open the French doors that led out to the terrace. Lennox paused to close the doors as an angry La Monica got right in his face and said in a controlled and muffled voice with his teeth clenched, "What the fuck happened?"

Lennox did not flinch and quickly replied, "It was the feds.... The FBI. From what I can tell, they confiscated account and transaction documents, and we think about 8 million in cash."

La Monica shouted, "Goddammit! How did this happen?"

Lennox answered, "I think they were tipped off and had someone on the inside. They had a court order with them, so it looks to me like they've been working on this for at least a couple of months."

Lennox leaned close to La Monica and said, "If Garrett didn't know about it, he should have."

La Monica was the boss and had great respect and faith in Lennox, and in that moment, he picked up on a small nuance in how Lennox said that to him and the look in his eyes as he did. It was something more than suspicion; Lennox knew who had betrayed them and perhaps even knew how it happened. La Monica knew what had to be done and that he needed to allow it to happen, so he simply told Lennox, "Take care of it."

Lennox nodded and responded in a low voice, "I have a plan."

As La Monica and Lennox reentered the office, the other four men were just arriving for the meeting and taking off their suit coats as they found their seats around the table. Lennox told the group, "We have a lot to cover so let's get started. I think better on my feet, so I'm going to keep moving as we talk."

Lennox started his walk around the table and said, "Yesterday, we lost 8 million dollars. The feds showed up with warrants in hand. Which could only mean that they were working on this for some time. There is no way that Livingston is either that good or that fucking lucky. I think he got some help."

La Monica slammed his hand down hard on the table and startled everyone as they all looked directly at him. The room fell completely silent as La Monica leaned forward on the table and looked to his left at Thomas Garrett. He stared angrily and asked, "What happened?" The loud noise surprised Garrett and caused his mind to wander. He had been constantly rehearsing his lie in his head and trying to look as calm as he could but now was thrown off and became visibly shaken and nervous. His face grew flush, and he started to sweat as he apologetically blurted out with his voice crackling, "I don't know, Boss. I really don't know."

Lennox had walked around the table and stopped directly behind Garrett. Lennox's right hand moved slowly inside his suit coat and retrieved his gun. The shiny barrel of the chrome-plated revolver emerged from the holster as he moved it smoothly to the back of Garrett's head. The muzzle flashed as a single shot rang out, and Garrett's body slumped onto the table as the two men seated directly across from him immediately pushed back in their chairs. They sat shocked and terrified with Garrett's blood and brain spattered across their faces and clothing. Lennox stated, "I don't know was the wrong answer."

Lennox leaned over Garrett's lifeless body and put both hands on the table as light smoke still rose from the barrel of the revolver under his right hand.

Lennox told the rest of them in a very loud and firm tone, "If the rest of you don't know what's going on in your banks, you better fucking find out. What happened yesterday will not happen again. Do you all understand me?" Lennox looked at each of the remaining men with a determined glare. No one said a word; they only sat, nodding in agreement. Lastly, Lennox told the two seated across from Garrett, "Now, you two, get yourselves cleaned up and get rid of this piece of shit."

Several minutes later, La Monica and Lennox sat on the terrace in the bright morning sunshine as the housekeeping staff cleaned the office. Lennox began to outline his plan to move forward and told La Monica, "I want to get our money out of Chicago. I've been giving this some thought, and it's a different world up here in Lake Forest. I think you once referred to it as a 'safe haven.' I think the locals up here will be far less likely to interfere or inquire about our activity, and I think we can use some of these new banks up this way to constantly move our money in and out of accounts, and even from bank to bank.

"We can create a kind of shell game that is far more sophisticated and much more difficult to track than what we've been doing. And even if we did encounter problems, with the money spread out among different accounts and even banks, our losses would be far less than the 8 million we lost yesterday."

Lennox continued, "I know someone at a bank near here. I'm going to call him today to set up a meeting. Give me a day or two, and I'll work out the details."

La Monica said, "Get something done this week."

Lennox replied, "I'll have something for you by Friday" as he grabbed his briefcase and turned to go.

La Monica walked a few steps behind him through the office and stood at the top of the stairs as he watched Lennox walk down.

La Monica shouted, "And get our money out of the banks today! I am not losing any more money." As his words echoed through the stairwell and hallway, Lennox had a determined look, and although he did not look back, he nodded slightly to himself in agreement.

CHAPTER 3

The Scheme

1957

Lennox sat in his car briefly and decided to just make the short drive to Grayslake for now to see his contact in person. Lennox, a determined and successful man, was seemingly unaffected by the fact that just about an hour earlier he shot a man in the head and ordered others to dispose of the body. He drove along narrow, two-lane country roads with cornfields on both sides that were only interrupted by the occasional gravel road used to access neighboring farms. His car slowed to cross over some very rough railroad tracks as he saw the sign that read, "Welcome to Grayslake, population 2,600."

Lennox drove into the newly developed downtown area, which was still a work in progress with many buildings still under construction. Still around were the feed depots, Farm & Fleets, and tractor supply stores. But now with sprinklings of new buildings and urban businesses scattered throughout. In the center of town was the largest of its new buildings, the Grayslake National Bank building. Lennox parked, pulled the lobby door open, and was immediately greeted by a very attractive young woman at the teller window. She saw him through the window in his very expensive car and expensive suit as he walked in. She quickly ran to the first teller station so she could be the one to say, "May I help you, sir?"

Lennox answered, "My name is Lennox. I'm here to see Allen Shaw."

She replied with a warm smile and lingering glance, "I'll let him know you are here, Mr. Lennox." She returned just a minute later. "Mr. Lennox, Mr. Shaw can see you now. If you would please follow me, I can show you to his office." Lennox followed as she looked back to smile at him several times before they arrived at Shaw's office.

Lennox was flattered by her attention and offered a polite smile in return but seemed unfazed by her flirting. He was used to this kind of attention from women and would not allow himself to be distracted. She announced, "Mr. Shaw, Mr. Lennox is here for you."

Shaw had started as a teller at a downtown Chicago bank used by Lennox years earlier. And had worked his way up to investment banker before he made the move to Grayslake with the promise of a promotion. Shaw was a man in his fifties and very tall and rail-thin. Shaw was a smart man but lacked sophistication and drive. He was good at his job but always seemed okay with just getting by with the bare minimum; he made no extra effort when it came to his appearance either. He had unusual and distinct short-gray hair with tight curls and wore thick, black-framed glasses that suited him well but to others appeared too big for his thin face. And although he had been promoted to bank president, he wasn't making the kind of money that other bank presidents did in Chicago. He still wore untailored off-the-rack suits. His appearance was at best described as acceptable, but Lennox was in a different category altogether and was always the best-dressed man in the room.

Shaw made his way from behind his desk and walked toward the door as he greeted Lennox with a handshake. "Hello, Aiden, it's been a long time." As he motioned for Lennox to come in and sit, he asked, "What brings you out this way?"

Lennox replied, "Allen, I'm on a tight schedule and don't have a lot of time, so let me get right to it. I am pulling all my money out of the city. Livingston has become a problem for us. I have an idea for something new, and you are my first stop. Now this idea does have some risk associated with it but also includes some significant incentives that could make you a very rich man."

Shaw was clearly intrigued and leaned forward in his chair, putting both elbows on his desk. "Tell me more."

Lennox closed the office door and, as he returned to Shaw's desk, opened his briefcase and said, "Yesterday, Livingston and the FBI seized about 8 million of my money."

Shaw interjected, "I heard about it on the news."

Lennox continued, "I'm in the process of taking our money out of our Chicago banks, and I want to move it up here into your bank."

Shaw interrupted, "Aiden, I'm not sure I can handle that much cash here."

Lennox put his palm up for Shaw to wait and be patient. "We will safeguard the money until we get this plan set up. I'm not dumping it on you today." He continued, "The first phase of this plan is that whatever we set up here in Grayslake, I will need you to help me make this same arrangement with another three or four banks in this area. Four banks may make things too complicated initially, so we'll start with three. We can add a fourth later if we need to. I want to bring you cash and then have you spread it out over your existing accounts and keep the money moving in random rotations to avoid detection from the feds. Then simultaneously, we will move money between banks periodically to accomplish the same thing."

Lennox paused and looked directly at Shaw. "Think of this as a large shell game. Each bank is a shell, and the cash is the pea."

Shaw asked, "With all of this cash coming in, can the bank use this money, or are we just keeping it hidden?"

Lennox replied, "Just use that old 'three-six-three' system you used to tell me so much about. You pay me 3 percent on my deposits, you lend our money out at 6 percent, and you'll be on the golf course by 3 p.m." Lennox smirked. "Isn't that how it goes? The banks can earn interest on every dollar they keep hidden, and each bank can decide whether they want to do that by investment or loan, but either way, I get my 3 percent."

Lennox told Shaw, "For being the first one in on this and helping me get this started, you will earn a monthly service stipend of $5,000 for every month that this plan continues undetected." Lennox reached into his briefcase and pulled out two bundles of cash, each of which was bound with a "$10,000" band. Lennox reached in for another two bundles. Then another. Until six bundles were neatly stacked in front of Shaw. "This is your first year paid upfront." Shaw's eyes lit up at the sight of all that money as Lennox said, "Any stipend arrangement that you need to make with any other bank presidents, or anyone else you need to help you with this, will need to come out of your end. I need your answer by the end of the day."

Shaw looked again at the big pile of cash in front of him and enthusiastically said, "I'm in. Let's get started."

Lennox walked to the door and, as he opened it, said, "Only share this with those you trust. I'll be in touch with you soon." Shaw was on board; he was not necessarily afraid of Lennox but knew that he was not someone to mess with or disappoint, so he had to do everything he could to make this work out. Shaw stood in the hallway and watched as Lennox's car drove out of view.

Shaw turned and walked toward Gordon Cain's office. Shaw had known Cain since his early days in banking and had hired him four years earlier as his replacement in the financial investment section when he was promoted to president. Cain was the same age as Shaw and about the same height, but Cain was much heavier, with shoulder-length, wavy gray hair.

He also had a rough complexion with deep pockmarks on his cheeks and neck caused by contracting chickenpox as a child. Though Cain was a very shrewd businessman and extremely good at money management and investment strategies, he lacked self-confidence, was extremely introverted, and became very uncomfortable in social settings. Any situation that required him to meet or talk to new people was difficult for him and caused anxiety. Because of his height, weight, glasses, complexion, hair, and general appearance Cain saw himself as unattractive and unappealing. However, over the last four years he had grown to know Shaw quite well, and they had become both reliable colleagues and good friends.

Shaw leaned into Cain's office and said, "Come with me."

Back at Shaw's office, Cain closed the door, and Shaw began to describe the plan that Lennox had just proposed.

After getting through the entire plan, Shaw reached into his desk drawer and pulled out one bundle of money from the stack that Lennox gave him. Shaw said, "This $10,000 is for your help in getting this started with me." Shaw continued to describe the amount of cash that could be moving through the bank, and Cain was quick to interject, "We don't have enough account holders to spread that much cash out and keep it undetected. And even if we could grow the number of accounts to do this, it will be a full-time job for me to make these rotations here, not to mention the movements between the other banks."

Shaw said, "Before we decide what we can't do, let's try to figure out what we can." They both recognized that they could not trust this plan with anyone else. It would need to be just the two of them.

Cain continued to break the plan down. "In order for us to manage that much cash coming in, the first thing we will need to do is significantly grow the number of our account holders so we can more effectively spread cash out over accounts.

"We will also need to find some creative ways to increase our exposure in the financial investment section so we can find more ways to address and explain losses. If we can show more in losses, it may help us offset undocumented money coming in." Cain continued, "We will need some help to accomplish this, and that person will need qualities that I just don't have. I mean, look at me, Allen. I can't bring this many new accounts into the bank. For us to generate the amount of new business this plan is going to require, we are going to need someone really special."

Cain walked over to the easel and flipped over to a clean sheet as he and Shaw started to brainstorm ideas.

Cain wrote furiously as they both shouted out adjectives… "Young, energetic, hardworking, charismatic, personable, attractive, honest, ambitious…"

Shaw added, "It wouldn't hurt if he was a Christian and maybe even a family man." So, Cain added those to the list as well before he paused a second to think before he wrote the last word on the list.

He wrote "naïve" and then emphatically drew circles around it.

Shaw asked, "What do you mean by that?"

Cain pointed at the list, moved his hand in a large circle around all the words that he had written, and said, "He needs to be all of these things, but he can't know too much about banking, or he may recognize some of the irregularities this plan is going to create. We don't need anyone asking too many questions about this."

Shaw stood with a worried look and placed his hand on his head, which he ran through his hair as he asked a very important question. "Where are we going to find someone to work in banking that doesn't know anything about banking?"

Cain let out a small grin as he said, "I may have a solution to that, but we need to go back to my office."

Cain grabbed his desktop Rolodex and started rifling through the cards before he found the one he was looking for and pulled it out firmly. It was the contact card of an old college classmate of his at the University of Wisconsin. She was currently working as the class administrator for the UW School of Banking in Madison.

Cain dialed his friend Meredith Ceja while Shaw sat and listened in.

Ceja answered the phone. "Hello."

The Scheme

Cain replied, "Meredith, it's Gordon Cain…"

Ceja responded, "Good morning, Gordon, how are you?"

"I'm doing well." Cain went on to say, "I'm working on a small project here in Grayslake and could use your help if you have a minute to talk."

"I do. What can I do to help you?"

"Does the School of Banking still do an entry-level banking program?" Cain asked.

Ceja replied, "Yes, we do a Level 103 class every summer."

"When does that next class start?"

"We have a class starting in two weeks on June 3."

Cain asked, "I know it's last minute, but is there any way you could get me enrolled in that class?"

"Gordon, this program is for people just getting started in banking. You're going to find yourself well overqualified for this class."

"It's really not for me," said Cain. "We are working on a plan to develop an internship program here in Grayslake, and I think that course could help me establish a baseline curriculum."

"Well, I could just print our curriculum and send it to you if that's easier," Ceja suggested.

"I appreciate that, but actually going through the program could help me get a better understanding of just what our interns would actually be going through here."

Ceja paused. "Okay, if that's what you really want to do. I would need you to pay the normal tuition, but I can pull a few strings and get you a spot in our next class if that's really what you want."

"Great, please send me the information, and I'll get you what you need to get me registered. Thank you, Meredith."

"You're welcome, Gordon. I'll reserve a spot for you

today, and I'll get this paperwork out in today's mail. Is there anything else?"

"No, I think that's it for now. Thanks, Meredith. Goodbye."

Shaw looked confused as he asked, "What was that all about?"

Cain asked him, "Do you think you can cover for me here on the investment side for a couple of months?"

"Sure, I guess so."

Cain replied, "Okay, then I am going to attend the summer course at the School of Banking at the University of Wisconsin that begins in a couple of weeks. There will be a couple hundred young students who are just starting out in banking in this class." Cain smiled as he told Shaw, "We'll find our guy in this class."

CHAPTER 4

The Chance Encounter

1957

It was a beautiful day in early June, and the University of Wisconsin campus was lush and green as Cain stood at the base of the steps to the School of Banking building. He looked up at the spires and took a nostalgic look at the other buildings as it had been just about thirty years since he was last on this campus. He found himself surrounded by young men making their way up the steps to check in for the ten-week Level 103 class. Cain took a deep breath, made his way up the stairs, and as he reached the top, was greeted by a sign that read "Registration" that directed him to the left door.

Cain entered and saw his old classmate, Meredith Ceja, seated at the long registration table. Ceja saw him, quickly rose, and moved around the table to greet him. Ceja was very active in school when they attended here and was a popular member of the best sorority on campus, Alpha Chi Omega. But she was also extremely smart and was elected to the class council and awarded Magna Cum Laude. After graduation she accepted her dream job of working for the university as an administrator and then worked her way into the School of Banking position she held now. She was successful, beautiful, and smart but had allowed herself to be consumed by her work and ambition. Being single at this point was not part of her plan and was the only part of her life that she wished were different. Her light olive skin tone complimented her Spanish heritage. She was tall and had a thin figure; her long legs were highlighted by her short, yellow print sundress and cute, strappy flat sandals. Her once-long chestnut brown hair was now cut shorter and in a flip hairdo paired with a yellow headband to keep hair off her face. Cain extended his right hand to shake hers, but she moved in close, intent on giving him a hug. Cain relented and they shared a rather clumsy and awkward embrace.

Ceja said, "It's been a long time."

Cain's face was flush; he was perspiring and still a bit out of breath from the climb up the stairs as he replied, "Too long. Thank you for doing this for me."

"Gordon, you're welcome," she replied. "If you need anything while you're here, just let me know. I am going to be the coordinator for this class as well, so I'll probably be seeing you quite a bit. Follow me over here, and I'll get you checked in."

Ceja led Cain back to her registration table, where she provided him with his welcome packet, which included his class schedule, class roster, and dormitory assignment of room 151 in Dickenson Hall. Before Ceja let Cain go, she told him, "We are holding an orientation for all the students, along with a campus tour. I realize that you know your way around campus, so you are not required to go if you don't want to. But if you do decide to, maybe we can grab a drink and catch up afterward?"

Cain awkwardly replied, "That sounds good, okay. Thanks again, Meredith." As Cain turned to search out his dorm room, he had already begun to feel overwhelmed and anxious at the prospect of having to find a way to interact with, and interview, all these young students. And now he had the added pressure of possibly meeting Ceja later. Cain made his way back down the many stairs as he continued to see a steady stream of young men making their way in from the parking lot and toward registration. As one of the young men passed him on his way up, he made eye contact with Cain and said, "Good morning, sir." Cain continued down another step or two before he suddenly stopped. He turned to look back at the young man and saw him taking two stairs at a time like he could not wait to get to the top. Cain watched him and thought about all the young men who had passed by him that day.

Very few had made eye contact with him, and none had offered any kind of personal interaction or greeting. Just that young man.

Cain decided to make his way back up the stairs and stood in line behind him. He listened as the young man chatted and made small talk with the woman checking him in. His conversation was funny, engaging, and seemingly effortless. Once he was finished checking in, Cain walked up next and asked the woman at the table, "What is the name of the young man you just checked in?"

She looked down briefly at her registration sheet and answered, "That was Wilmer Hays."

Cain said, "Thank you very much" as he turned to his right to seek out Ceja again.

Ceja saw him coming and asked, "Gordon, is something wrong?"

Cain answered, "No, nothing. But there is a student registered for this class named Wilmer Hays. We just ran into each other outside and realized that our families are old friends. Is there any way you could change the dorm assignments to have us room together?"

Ceja checked her sheet and told Cain, "His roommate has not checked in yet so I can just switch you into his room. You will be in 205 now. Is there anything else?"

He answered, "No, thanks again, Meredith. See you later."

Cain made the short drive around to Dickenson Hall and made his way up to room 205, where he found a room that felt much smaller than it had all those years ago. Each room was set up with two twin beds, two small desks, and two small closets. Cain found the room a bit stuffy, so he cracked the window open and left the door standing open to allow some breeze to flow through. Since he was the first to arrive, he chose his bed and began to hang some items in his closet.

A few minutes later, and although the door was open, Cain heard someone knock on it and turned to see the same young man who said "Good morning" to him on the stairs a short time earlier.

The young man entered the room, dropped his suitcase, and extended his right hand while introducing himself. "I'm Wilmer Hays. Call me Will."

Will was a good-looking young man and clean-shaven, with what some would describe as a baby face that made him appear much younger than his age. He had dark eyes and full, wavy black hair, thick on top, combed back neatly, and trimmed shorter on the sides. Will was a former Marine, so he was physically fit and exhibited great posture. He was self-confident but paired that with the charm of someone much shorter in stature. If he were six-feet-two, some might have thought he was cocky. Cain shook his hand and introduced himself. "My name is Gordon Cain." Cain pointed at his bed and told Will, "I went ahead and grabbed this bed and this closet."

Will smiled and graciously and gladly accepted his accommodations by saying, "Great, I'll take these."

During the walk back to the auditorium, Will drove the conversation with small talk, comments about the campus, and the weather. Will had a smooth gait, making effortless strides as they walked. Cain struggled with the pace and was out of breath, perspiring and doing all he could to keep up before finally asking Will to slow down a little. Will felt like he was the one who needed to keep the conversation going because of the two of them, he was clearly more comfortable in the conversation and was confident speaking on most any topic. Although Cain was apprehensive about meeting new people, he found Will to be quite genuine and non-judgmental and very quickly found himself at ease with him.

As they entered the auditorium and found seats together, Will paused before he sat to take a quick visual inventory of this class of 140 students now seated inside.

Will saw that most in attendance were like him, in their mid-to-late twenties or early thirties, and that Cain was clearly the oldest in the class. As Ceja walked to the podium to introduce herself as the class coordinator, Cain heard several muffled catcalls from some of the men in the rows behind him and thought that she really was very attractive and probably way too good-looking to ever be with him. So, when the orientation concluded, Cain walked over to meet Ceja by the stage. She greeted him with a big smile, and her body language indicated that she was happy to see him as he told her, "Meredith, it's been a long day. I think I'm going to pass on that drink and just head back to my room." Her smile diminished a bit, but she did not let on that she was disappointed and simply said, "Okay. We can do it another time. Like I said earlier, we'll be seeing each other a lot over the next ten weeks."

On the first day of classes, Will, like most of the others in the class, found himself a little out of his depth when it came to certain terminology and theories. Cain, however, seemed to have a decent grip on what was being discussed, and as the first week came to an end, it was clear to Will that Cain possessed quite a bit of knowledge and experience in the banking world. He also noticed that although Cain wasn't eager to raise his hand to answer questions or participate in class discussions, he would mumble the correct answers under his breath. Cain was also the only student in the class who wasn't taking any notes or even following along in the textbooks or course pack.

It became obvious to most in the class that Cain was different from the rest of them, but Will was impressed by Cain and saw him as an asset to achieving success in the program. Others in the class tried desperately to position themselves for study and project groups with Will and Cain, but the pair would typically stick to themselves.

Each day after classes, Will and Cain grabbed dinner together in the cafeteria before heading back to their dorm room to study and complete homework assignments for the next day.

The current day's lectures and course assignments would dominate Will's attention on most nights, but when schoolwork was completed, Cain and Will would talk for hours until lights out. Cain was there to identify and interview any candidate who could help him achieve his goal, so Cain needed to learn as much about Will as he could. Cain asked questions about every aspect of Will's life and experiences. He had already discovered that Will was a great storyteller and found the added benefit of being entertained by what he was learning about him.

Will and Cain both settled comfortably to talk in what would now become their usual spots. Cain chose his desk chair while Will found himself more comfortable on the floor and used the side of his bed as a backrest. Cain wanted to learn more about Will's past, so he asked, "What was life for you like as a kid?"

Will looked up to the ceiling as he thought back...

Franklin Grove, Illinois, Sunday, May 17, 1936

It was a sunny and warm afternoon, and a small white farmhouse with green shingles sat atop a shallow hill that provided nice views of the surrounding fields, pastureland, and valley. A line of mature oak trees and full evergreen shrubs protected the west side of the house from the wind while the freshly painted white dairy barn and adjoining milk house protected the house from the south. Just behind the milk house were two tall concrete block grain silos with silver tin roofs that matched the barn and the milk house.

The small Hays family farm was just what you would expect to see on a postcard or a painting by Donald Hughes. At just about 120 acres, it was well cared for and beautifully maintained. The acreage was just about evenly divided between cornfields and pastureland, and two horses were corralled between the front of the house and the main road.

To the east of the house, a small grove of woods provided shelter for all types of wild berries to grow and for the occasional deer to be spotted and chased by the kids.

On this Sunday afternoon, the Hays family had just returned from church as their 1929 Ford AA pickup truck kicked up dust along the dirt driveway before coming to a stop in front of the house. Before the doors of the truck could even swing open, three of the four kids sitting in the pickup bed hopped over the side and ran from the truck, unleashing the pent-up energy from both the church service and the long ride home. One of the older girls circled back after realizing that her youngest brother would need help getting out of the truck. She lifted him and then set him down, and he ran to catch up with the others as Eugene, the oldest at age eight, suggested to his sisters and younger brother, Will (now five years old), that they all play a game of hide and seek before they would be called inside for dinner. Eugene took young Will by the hand and led him over to the barn as he told him, "If you can find a hiding place in here that no one can find you in, then you will win the game, and the next time we are at the store, I'll ask Mom to buy you an ice cream cone." Will smiled while looking up at his big brother and said, "Okay, Eugene" as Eugene slid the large barn door closed and left Will alone in the darkness.

With the only light provided by a small glass pane on the door next to the milk-holding tanks, Will found his way to a back corner where the barn cats would sometimes hide.

He could hear Eugene outside counting, "One, two…" and so on until he reached "Ten. Ready or not, here I come." Will sat quietly in the darkness and tried desperately to not make any sound that would give away his location. The minutes passed, and at just five years old, he did not yet fully understand time and did not realize that hours were ticking by. He sat alone in the darkness until about 5 p.m. when the rest of the kids were called inside for dinner. As they took their places around the kitchen table, his mother asked, "Has anyone seen Wilmer?"

Hearing that, Eugene busted out laughing and said, "I told him when we got home from church that we were going to play hide and seek. I told him to go hide in the barn, but I never went to look for him. What a dumbass." Eugene continued laughing as the oldest of the girls jumped from her seat and directed a nasty glare at Eugene before running out the door as she called out for Will.

She struggled to slide open the heavy barn door and called out to Will in the darkness. He answered back to her by asking, "Did I win?" She followed the sound of his voice and found him still sitting alone in the dark corner. She asked, "Are you okay?" He stood up and for a brief second was happy to see his sister, but then looked down in embarrassment at his wet pants. "Oh, honey, why didn't you go to the outhouse if you had to go potty?" Will answered, "Eugene told me he would ask Mommy to buy me an ice cream if nobody could find me." His sister shook her head in disgust at Eugene and said lovingly, "Come on, come on out of there. Let's get you changed and cleaned up for dinner." She took Will by the hand and walked him out the barn door as she pulled hard on the door to close it, leaving the darkness behind them.

Will looked down at the floor as he finished that story. Cain responded, "Will, that's a terrible story. What did your father do about that?"

Will looked puzzled as he said, "Nothing. Not a thing. Eugene was Dad's favorite, and it did not matter what I did. In my father's eyes, I was never going to measure up to him." That prompted Will to remember another story...

Franklin Grove, Illinois, Saturday, September 18, 1941

A constant haze of dust filled the air from tractors working in nearby fields. It was harvesting time on the Hays farm, and Will, now ten years old, was working alone in the dairy barn cleaning out stalls. On this warm day, he was covered in sweat as he shoveled manure and straw with his small pitchfork into the waiting wheelbarrow nearby. He was wearing hand-me-down bib overalls that were faded, tattered, and getting a bit tight even for his small frame. Under his overalls was a plain white undershirt that looked as if it hadn't been washed in a week. He moved awkwardly, yet deliberately, wearing large rubber boots with metal buckles that didn't seem to keep them tight enough on his small feet. The boots belonged to his dad and were at least five sizes too big for him.

The cool darkness inside the barn was suddenly interrupted when the barn door slid open and warm air and bright sunshine flooded in. Will looked toward the door and squinted as the light hit his eyes. In the doorway was the silhouette of Eugene, now thirteen, and against the bright background, he yelled out, "Hey, dumbass, Dad needs oil for the tractor, so go grab two quarts and run it out to him, and hurry up, he's waiting."

Will dropped his pitchfork and yelled back, "Okay, Eugene" as he ran as quickly as he could in the oversized boots to the storage cabinet in the back of the barn, then grabbed two cans of motor oil and the filler spout before he ran off toward the field where his dad was working.

Will was running as fast as he could while holding the filler spout in his right hand and pressing the two quarts of oil to his chest with his forearm. As he ran, one loose-fitting boot flew off his small right foot and spun into the air in his wake. Not slowing down, he continued in his sock until the other boot came loose, the same as the first. He kept running in his socks until he arrived at the tractor. Will was a little out of breath but had on a slight smile as he thought that he had made pretty good time and his dad would be pleased.

Will found his dad sitting in the shade behind one of the large back wheels of the tractor, and before he could even get out a "Hi, Dad," his father barked out, "Goddammit, Wilmer, what the hell took you so long? You need to move quicker, boy. Why can't you be more like your brother?"

Will answered, "Eugene told me you needed this oil, so I ran as fast as I could, and I even lost my boots along the way."

His dad took the oil from his arms and, as he turned away, said, "You better find those boots, boy. I'm not buying another pair. You'll be mucking those stalls in your bare feet."

As young Will walked back to the barn, he had his head down and was dejected as he scanned left and right along the way, trying to find his boots in the tall grass. As he passed Eugene walking back to the tractor, he noticed that he was wearing clean boots, clean blue jeans, and a clean dry shirt and didn't appear to have a drop of sweat on him.

As Eugene passed, he took a sip of his cold drink and said, "Back to the shit, dumbass." Will found the first of his boots, picked it up, and carried it with him to the next boot.

Then he sat down in the tall grass and pulled on both boots as he looked back over his shoulder to see Eugene climbing up on the tractor to ride along with his dad. Will walked back to the barn with his head down as he tried to hold back his tears. He reached up with both hands, grabbed the door handle, and pulled the heavy barn door with all his might as he closed himself back inside the darkness.

CAIN WAS QUICK TO REACT TO THAT AND SAID, "THAT STORY was worse than the first one. How long did all that go on?"

Will answered, "My whole life. Every day of my childhood had some version of that story in it. That is until… I'll never forget this day." And he thought back again…

Rockton, Illinois, Saturday, August 31, 1946

Will had just celebrated his fifteenth birthday, and today, he was working in the hay loft. He stood at the edge of the open loft door, some twenty feet above the ground, in a pair of blue jeans, black boots, and a tight, plain white t-shirt with the sleeves cut off. He was pulling hay bales off the wagon below using a hook and pulley. The process was perfectly choreographed with Will standing in the hay loft opening, guiding the rope up and down with his left hand. He lowered the hook to Eugene who waited on the wagon below and pulled the rope to hook the next bale. Eugene would then signal his father on the tractor to pull the rope and elevate the bale to Will.

Once the bale was high enough, Will would swing the bale in through the loft door and then lower it to the floor as his father backed up the tractor to release the rope's tension. All of that occurred in a well-orchestrated and smooth motion as each part happened in a simultaneously choreographed routine. Will unhooked each bale and grabbed the cords with both hands to stack them neatly before he sent the hook back down to the wagon for the next bale.

His dad drove the tractor back and forth to raise and lower the rope while Eugene, on the hay wagon, had selected the much easier task of hooking bales.

Will worked quickly to keep up with the bales being sent up to him. Sweat dripped from his forehead and started to soak through his shirt; his sweat-covered arms were now becoming more muscular and defined as he tossed the bales onto stacks up to six high. While still smaller in stature, it was evident that Will was growing into a young man.

Again, the darkness inside the barn was interrupted when the barn door slid open. This time, the silhouette of Eugene yelled up to the loft, "Hey, dumbass, that's the last bale. Come down when you're done stacking those." Will offered up the usual, "Okay, Eugene," but this time he added just a touch of a sarcastic tone, which made him smile as he wiped the sweat from his forehead and ran his hands through his wet hair. He walked to the hole cut out of the loft floor, climbed down the hand-made, and now well-worn, ladder of cut two-by-fours on the barn wall, and jumped down from the second wrung. As his feet hit the dirt, he turned around and found Eugene standing right in his face as he asked, "So, you think you're tough now? Huh?" as he gave Will a push on the chest, forcing him back a step or two. "Just remember, dumbass, you'll never be as good as me. You'll never be as tough as me, and now, dumbass, you're going to be stuck here without me."

Will responded, "What do you mean?"

Eugene told Will, "A recruiter came to school yesterday, and I joined the Marine Corps. Mom and Dad signed off on it today, so when I turn eighteen, I'm out of here."

Will stood there quietly and paused for just a second or two, letting that news sink in. He did not respond; he simply walked past Eugene toward the barn door. Will felt that he had somehow managed to survive his childhood, and now with Eugene leaving, he could enjoy a brief respite before he too had to find his way out of life on the farm.

In that moment, Will also felt a surge of purpose and self-confidence and thought that he would do everything he could to prove to Eugene and his father that he was tough and would be successful someday. As Will stood in the barn doorway, he looked back at Eugene as he reached out to grab the barn door. Now, with very little effort, he slowly began to pull the barn door closed. This time, and finally, he left Eugene standing alone in the darkness.

CHAPTER 5

The Threat

1957

It was another clear and warm morning in June as Mike Baker stood at his post at the front gates of the La Monica estate's front gates. He saw a car turn from the main road onto the long gravel driveway and checked his wristwatch; it was 8:40 a.m. A beat-up 1953 Dodge Coronet with celery-green paint traveling fast kicked up dust as it sped toward the gate. The car began to slow as it approached and came to an abrupt stop as the large cloud of dust continued past it. The driver rolled down his window and said, "I'm Allen Shaw, and I have a nine o'clock meeting with Mr. Lennox and Mr. La Monica." Baker waved his hand in front of his face to clear the dust away and seemed more than a bit perturbed with the speed at which the driver had approached before replying, "They're expecting you, sir. Go on in." He then motioned to his partner to open the gate.

Shaw drove into the front circle and parked his car next to Lennox's vehicle; as he walked to the front door, he looked back briefly and seemed a little embarrassed to leave his car next to Lennox's, which was so clean and expensive. Shaw was met at the front door by the butler who directed him down the hallway and up the stairs, where Shaw found

Lennox and La Monica already seated in the office. Lennox stood to greet Shaw with a handshake while La Monica knew that he didn't need to stand up to meet anyone and remained seated. Shaw walked over to La Monica, extended his hand, and said, "Mr. La Monica, it's very nice to meet you, sir. Thank you for inviting me to your beautiful home."

La Monica was all business and said, "Aiden has been telling me about this plan of his. Why don't you tell us what's happening on your end?"

Shaw sat down and leaned forward in his seat. "When Aiden first came to me in May, we talked about the idea of using my bank to keep your money hidden. For us to spread that much cash out over our accounts effectively, we will need to dramatically increase the number of our account holders. Cain and I have decided that we will need to hire someone to help us do that. We also believe it will be safer for all of us if this new hire doesn't know what we are doing. One of our primary concerns is that this plan will create some irregularities, and frankly, we can't afford to have anyone asking too many questions. So, Gordon Cain is going to spend the next ten weeks at a summer banking program at the University of Wisconsin in Madison where there will be a large pool of potential candidates that we can choose from to help us with our needs."

La Monica, agitated, slammed his hand down on the table and yelled, "Ten weeks? Are you telling me your plan is going to take ten weeks to get started?"

Shaw was startled by this and even a little scared, but he managed to calmly reply, "Our plan requires someone special that has tremendous people and communication skills. We can't waste any time getting this started, so for us to see immediate results, we also need him to be hard-working, dedicated, and ambitious. Once we get this going in our bank, we will probably need to add someone like this in the other banks as well. The more accounts we can add, the more cash we can manage.

"Cain will be making all the cash movements and rotations and will also integrate some creative losses both on our investment balance sheet and our P&Ls. He thinks that should help offset any cash that comes in before or after account rotations. We might even be able to float some of the larger amounts between the fed branches to buy ourselves a week or two if we are in a pinch. Cain is a very bright guy and a great money manager. This is a good plan. We can do this."

La Monica had paid close attention to every word Shaw said as he leaned forward. Then he looked directly at Shaw and said, "I understand that you know Aiden, and I know that Aiden trusts you with this idea. But if you fuck us on this deal, I'll kill you myself. Do you understand me?"

Shaw looked La Monica in the eye and said with confidence, "You can trust us. We can do this."

La Monica got up, put his hand on Shaw's shoulder, and said, "You better be sure of that, and you better not forget it." Then he walked out of the office.

Lennox asked, "So ten weeks?"

Shaw answered, "Cain started June 3, so we should be ready for your first cash drop sometime in August."

Lennox stood and said, "Okay, August it is."

Shaw stood to leave, but before he got out the door, Lennox stopped him by saying, "He's right, you know."

Shaw looked back and asked, "What is that?"

Lennox slid both hands into his pants pockets and, while looking very confident, relaxed, and at ease, said, "If you fuck this up, he will kill you."

CHAPTER 6

The Monologue

1957

On another particularly warm July evening, Cain and Will were again in their dorm room chatting. The window was cracked open to allow some breeze to enter, which caused the curtains to move gently. The only light, provided by the desk lamp behind Cain, bounced off the curtains and appeared to "flicker" throughout the room. With Cain seated in his desk chair, Will again chose the floor, and as Will began to sit, he pulled up slightly on the front pleats of his trousers to provide extra room in his inseam to not rip the crotch of his pants as he lowered himself. Cain recognized that and thought that this was no ordinary farm kid. Will exhibited a certain sense of sophistication in his mannerisms uncommon for someone in his age group and from his background.

Cain asked, "So, Will, how did you decide to get into banking?"

Will took a deep breath and prepared himself for tonight's monologue. "You remember that I told you that my brother finally left for the Marines? Well, I knew I would probably do the same after I graduated, so I enlisted and went to boot camp at Pendleton. My first assignment was in the office of Staff Sergeant Robert Christian who oversaw a staff of nineteen of us. We coordinated all the civilian and enlisted housing on base. It was a good job, and after just a few weeks, Christian invited me to join a mentoring program. That's when I began to get noticed for excelling in accounting and office management skills.

"So, after just about nine months, he put me in for a promotion to corporal, and it was Christian that suggested banking might be something I could do after my military service. So, when I got out, Carol and I moved back to Illinois, and I got a job at our hometown bank in LaSalle. And the rest as they say is history."

Cain asked, "You mentioned Carol. Is that your wife?"

Will's face lit up and he smiled. "Yes, she's my wife. But Gordon, she's more than that, she's my whole life."

Cain asked, "How did you meet?"

Will answered, "Now that is a good story." And he offered a big smile and thought back to that day...

LaSalle, Illinois, Tuesday September 5, 1949

Lasalle Peru High School was the largest high school in the entire county, and for Will, it was unlike any school he had ever seen. With three stories of red brick and limestone façade, it was equally huge and magnificent. The clock tower in its center reached up another story and a half and had adjoining limestone spires that resembled something you might see on a church in a faraway foreign country.

On the first day of school, there was a lot of activity as some students rushed to get inside while others were catching up with friends they hadn't seen since last year. The parking lot began to fill with cars parked by older kids and parents just dropping kids off at the door. Conversations around campus were interrupted as an old beat-up farm truck pulled into the parking lot. With no muffler, the truck was loud and burned so much oil that a haze of blue smoke poured out of the exhaust pipe like a genie leaving the bottle. As the truck turned into the lot, groups that had gathered there quickly headed into the school to escape the blue cloud of noxious exhaust chasing them. Word quickly made its way through the halls as everyone wondered who was driving that crappy truck.

Will slid out of the truck wearing a plain, white dress shirt, black slacks, and black dress shoes. His sisters had given him a fresh haircut the night before and had picked out clothes for him to wear: the same outfit he typically wore to church on Sundays. Will joked with his sisters before he left that he thought he looked like a "teenage preacher." But he was going to put his best foot forward and made the long and lonely walk into his new school to start his senior year.

Will pulled the front door open and found the hallways packed with kids as he tried to make his way through the crowd. He apologetically bumped into strangers and tried his best to weave through the crowd when out of nowhere, a girl grabbed his arm and literally dragged him across the hallway to her locker where her friend stood waiting. She got right in his face and with all kinds of attitude asked, "Who are you?"

Will, caught a bit off-guard by this, was nervous as he offered a short but simple, "Will."

The girl chimed right back, "Nice to meet you, 'Willy.' I'm Margie and this is my friend CJ."

CJ extended her hand to Will and said, "Hi, I'm Carol. Just call me Carol."

Margie was a cute girl but shorter than Will and a genuine firecracker. She was high-energy, funny, and boisterous. If she didn't get attention from boys, she would make them pay attention by being funny, outgoing, and direct. Margie wore a red ribbon in her short brown hair, and her round face was accented by her rosy cheeks and bright red lipstick. She was dressed nicely in a white blouse, a red-and-black plaid skirt, ankle socks, and black flats.

Margie was the perfect muse for Carol who, on the other hand, was about Will's height and thin and athletic. Carol was a singer and dancer who was comfortable performing on stage in school musicals.

But she was a bit more reserved and composed, and added small touches of shyness in meeting new boys. Carol also exhibited a little more style, choosing to wear a light blue ribbon in her long, wavy brown hair that matched her light blue blouse. She paired that with a dark blue cardigan sweater with distinct, ornamental light blue stitching. Both of which perfectly matched her blue pleated skirt. And her entire outfit was accented by her bobby socks, tan saddle shoes, and tan clutch.

Will stood there in the hallway unable to take his eyes off Carol as he said, "It's nice to meet you both, but let me get this straight. You are Margie [as he pointed at Margie], and CJ is Carol [as he pointed at Carol], but now [he pointed to himself] I have to live with being called 'Willy' for the rest of the year?" Will shook his head while feigning annoyance. Margie and Carol laughed at that, and as they headed to their first class, Will overheard Carol say, "Well, he's cute."

Back in the dorm room, Will said, "After that first day, we spent as much time together as we possibly could. Carol was always busy with chorus, dance, or school plays, so I would sometimes just sit in the empty seats of the auditorium after school and watch her practice. That would make me late getting home for afternoon chores, but at this point, I didn't care. She was worth it. She was beautiful, talented, and sweet. I had never met a girl like her before, and I would just sit there completely mesmerized by her smile, her voice, and the way she moved on stage.

"That whole year went by like a blur for me, and we were inseparable. We spent all our time together and enjoyed doing the simplest of things.

"Whether we were taking in a movie at the drive-in, sharing a burger at the malt shop, or just sitting together under our favorite tree talking and laughing until all hours, we shared every detail of our lives and learned everything we needed to know about each other. She told me that her friends had called her CJ since middle school, but that when she met me, she wanted me to simply know her as Carol. She told me that after that day, she didn't allow anyone to call her CJ again. I told her that my first impression of her was that because her outfit looked expensive, I thought she was probably a typical rich girl. You know…superficial, snobby, and spoiled. And boy was I wrong. The more I got to know her, the more I found that she was none of those. For as pretty, talented, and smart as she was, it was her generous spirit and kindness toward others that set her apart from any other girl I had ever known.

"And even though her family did have money, she was more down to earth than any other person I knew. She shared every detail of her childhood and life with me. Even her deepest feelings about how difficult it was for her to be without her father who died when she was just six years old. And then when she needed her mother the most, she was sent to spend more and more time with her grandparents because her mother needed to go back to work. She cherished the time she had with her grandparents. I think that was when Carol began to learn the importance of family, and that is why love of family is the biggest priority in her life today.

"Then one day, amid all the chaos going on in their lives, her mother met a man named Paul Coates.

"Paul was a widower and the son of a prominent doctor in town. In addition to being tall and handsome, he was polished, educated, and charismatic. Carol also learned that he was an accomplished musician who played the violin.

"Carol was so excited to have someone in her life who shared her interest and love of music. She shared stories of those early years as a young girl sitting on the piano bench next to her mother as she played duets with Paul. Carol would join in with them, singing and dancing for hours on end, and felt the pure joy of those special moments. She credited moments like those for fostering her love of performing. Carol was overjoyed just a year or so later when Paul and her mother got married.

"Carol said that both of their lives were instantly better and that he showed Carol love, encouragement, and support. But all of that changed the following year when her mother gave birth to her brother, Henry. Of course, Carol loved her little brother, and although she still felt love from both her parents, she sensed that something was different. She confessed to me that she felt shuffled back to second place, a feeling that I knew quite well and could empathize with her over.

"Carol told me that as she grew older, Henry received all the help from tutors and was provided music lessons. For as smart and talented as Carol was, she was never offered any extra attention. Paul seemed to put all his focus on his son's success, leaving nothing for her. Paul also set very high expectations for Henry and wanted him to attend an Ivy League school, though no one discussed higher education with Carol at all.

"That meant any money Paul and her mother set aside for college would be reserved for Henry. Carol said that she did not resent Paul because that was just the way he was raised. His father had done those same things for him when he was young, so Carol convinced herself that it was just the way it was, and there was nothing she could do about it.

"It became increasingly evident to her that she would need to be the one responsible for creating her own life.

"If she truly was disappointed by any of that, she never let those feelings show through. She grew into a genuine, caring, and happy young woman more determined than ever to take control and create her own life narrative."

CHAPTER 7

The Smoke

1957

It had been a clear and dry summer, and this warm July morning was no different than the others; the same caravan of black sedans was again making its way through the streets of Chicago. They came to a stop in front of the Chicago National Bank at the intersection of Clark and Lake streets.

The first agent pushed through the front door of the bank and announced boldly, "FBI... Don't anyone move. We have a search warrant." The remaining agents rushed past him in what was now a well-planned and rehearsed order and began moving tellers away from their windows and frightened customers to safety. As other bank staff were relocated to empty offices off the lobby, the bank president emerged from his office.

In his late forties and short, overweight, and nearly bald with just small patches of dark hair above his ears, the man had a full, round face accented by thick brown eyebrows, a thick brown mustache, and thick cheeks, with an equally thick neck and jowls. His brown, plaid three-piece suit looked a size too small for his large frame, and he walked toward the agents in what looked like an exaggerated waddle as he introduced himself in a deep voice, "Gentlemen, I'm Jack Higgins. I am the president of this bank. What can I do for you?"

The agent responded, "We have a search warrant, and we expect your complete cooperation."

Higgins smiled and said, "My staff and I will get you whatever you need."

Hours passed, after which the bank interior grew calm and quiet since no new customers were permitted to enter.

It was just after noon as Livingston arrived on location, confidently walked into the bank, and flashed his credentials to the uniformed Chicago police officer stationed at the front door. The lead agent saw Livingston arrive and greeted him just inside the front door as he grabbed his elbow, pulled him aside, and said, "Sam, there's nothing here. No cash, no records. It's all gone." Livingston's face turned red. He was now disappointed and visibly angry.

He looked over his right shoulder and saw Higgins leaning back in his chair with his feet up on the desk. Higgins smiled from the corner of his mouth as his lips were still wrapped around his cigar. Smoke rose as he sat with his arms crossed in quiet confidence as Livingston walked over to him, knocked his feet off the desk, leaned in close to his face, and said, "You knew we were coming, didn't you, you son of a bitch?"

Higgins never gave up the menacing grin and whispered back to Livingston, "Mr. Livingston, I didn't vote for you, and I don't like you, so I have no problem saying this to you... Go fuck yourself," right before blowing a mouth full of cigar smoke in Livingston's face.

Livingston turned back to the FBI agents and said, "They knew we were coming. Let's go. Get everybody out."

CHAPTER 8

The Questions

1957

Back in Will and Cain's dorm room, their conversation continued as Cain asked, "So you married your high school sweetheart?"

Will answered, "Well, I graduated in '50, but Carol was still just a junior, so when I went off to the Marines, she stayed behind to finish school. She graduated that following summer in 1951."

Will remembered back to that day...

> LaSalle, Illinois, Saturday, June 2, 1951
> LaSalle-Peru High School
>
> It was a beautiful, sunny, and warm Saturday afternoon on the front lawn of the school. Bright blue skies above and lush green grass below provided the perfect contrast to the thousands of white folding chairs arranged neatly in rows in front of the large stage, which used the front of the school as a backdrop.
>
> Families and guests were filing in for the graduation ceremony for the class of 672 seniors, scheduled to start in an hour. The LaSalle-Peru Cavaliers

school colors were green and red, and with so many students mingling about in red and green caps and gowns, the festivities had a bit of a Christmas in June feeling. As they made their way to their seats, Will asked Paul if he could have a quick word with him in private. Paul did not want to walk too far from Sally and Henry, so he just turned to Will and asked quietly, "What is it?"

Will said in a quiet reply, "I'm flying back to Pendleton tomorrow morning, and I would like to ask Carol to marry me tonight. Can I have your permission to do that?"

Paul smiled and answered, "Yes, Will, you have our permission. We would like nothing more. I appreciate you asking for our blessing."

The ceremony began, and with such a large class, a seemingly endless list of names that Will did not know were called. So, he sat back, daydreamed, and found ways to distract himself as he waited for Carol's name to be announced. As the list went on, he noticed that her row of students had started to make their way toward the stage. Carol searched the crowd, saw Will first, gave him a big smile, and blew him a kiss. As her name was read aloud, Carol walked across the stage, received her diploma, and paused briefly to hug her drama and chorus teachers before having her picture taken. She waved from the stage to her parents before returning to her seat.

As the ceremony concluded, Will handed Sally a folded note and asked, "Would you please give this to Carol when you see her? I have a couple of things I need to do to get ready."

After the last name was called, the principal congratulated the "Class of 1951," and all the graduates tossed their caps high into the air in celebration. After spending a few minutes with Margie and her other friends, Carol caught up with her parents and was visibly disappointed that Will had already left. Sally handed Carol a note that read, "I love you and I'm proud of you. I needed to leave early, but please meet me at our tree at sunset." Once home, Carol quickly changed her clothes and rushed back out the door, not wanting to miss the sunset on this beautiful day.

Carol knew that "our tree" was the large oak tree where they had spent hours together and was a spot that only the two of them knew about. Will arrived at the tree early and was pacing back and forth to burn off some nervous energy as the sun was just starting to sink into the western sky. He saw a cloud of dust in the distance from Carol's car driving down the gravel and dirt road and got himself into position.

Will was wearing his Marine Corps blue dress uniform and stood at attention. Carol saw him from a distance and began running toward the tree. Will watched her as if she was running in slow motion. Her long brown hair billowed in the wind, and she wore her favorite pale blue floral sundress. Her beautiful smile was highlighted by her bright red lipstick.

His eyes began to well up with emotion as he had never seen anything more beautiful than Carol at that moment. Carol leaped into his arms and squeezed him around his neck as he whispered in her ear, "I love you. I'm not sure I'll ever be able to tell you how much."

Carol whispered back, "I know. I love you too."

Will looked into Carol's eyes and said, "I have to fly back tomorrow, and there is something that I just can't wait to ask you." Will stood in front of Carol and slowly lowered to one knee, then presented her with a ring and asked, "Will you marry me?"

Carol cried out with an immediate, "Yes."

Will continued, "We got married that August, and the next day we packed everything we had in the car and headed back to California."

Cain interjected, "That's a great story. You know, I lived in California for a little while too. I was there until I turned five. That's when my dad took a job in Illinois, and we moved to Waukegan." Will was surprised to hear Cain share any details about his life. Usually, Will did all the talking, so Will encouraged Cain to open up by saying, "Tell me more."

Cain continued, "Then when I was seven, my parents were killed in an auto accident."

Will, still sitting on the floor, reached out to Cain and put his hand on his knee. "I'm so sorry, Gordon."

"Thanks, Will, I appreciate that, but it was a long time ago. I'm okay now." He continued, "After that, it was just me and my sisters. We lived with my grandparents, but it really was my sisters that raised me. And as I got older, I found myself getting into more and more trouble. I wasn't necessarily looking for trouble, but it always seemed to have a way of finding me. If you know what I mean. My sisters did the best they could with me, but I made it hard on them. No doubt, harder than it had to be.

"So, when I turned eighteen, I knew I needed to get out of there, so I joined the Army. I knew I needed to go; it was my only real chance to get out of Waukegan. I wasn't going to let my sisters be responsible for me as an adult the way they were when I was a kid. They needed a break from me. The Army gave me a chance to grow up and convinced me that I needed an education. So, when I got out, I picked UW Madison because it was close enough to my sisters that I could get to them when I needed to but also far enough away that I wouldn't have to worry about them just stopping by every week."

Will smiled at that and said, "I know what you mean. I have two sisters too." Then he asked, "Did you ever get married?"

"Yes, I was married to Carrie for ten years… Eight of them were good. The last two not so much. We've been divorced for about five years now."

"Any kids?" asked Will.

"No, thank God for that."

Will inquired, "You think you'll ever try again?"

Cain shook his head. "Nope. No more for me. Once was enough."

Will offered some encouragement. "Gordon, you never know what God has planned for you. You should stay positive and be open to meeting new people. You never know when you could meet someone really great."

"Thanks, Will. You are kind to say that, but I think I had my one chance, and I messed it up."

Will was growing very fond of his new friend Cain and was beginning to view him as the male role model he never had but always wanted. As time went by, he began to see Cain more as a mentor and father figure than just a classmate.

It was August now, and the course schedule was winding down. Will and Cain had spent so much time together that Cain knew almost everything he needed to about Will. He had grown quite fond of Will and was convinced that he was exactly what they needed in Grayslake. Cain was waiting for just the right opening to make his pitch when Will finally asked the question, "What's Grayslake like?"

Cain knew this was his opportunity, so he adjusted his posture and tried his best to emulate Will by raising his level of enthusiasm; although uncomfortable, he did his best to be animated and demonstrative in his presentation. He told Will, "Where should I start? Grayslake is a beautiful area. You would love it there. It is the fastest-growing suburb in all of Lake County, and what makes it unique is that it is a new and progressive farming community. And when I say, 'farming community,' I mean our downtown is literally surrounded by working farms, and it is still not unusual to see a tractor or combine drive slowly through town on its way to a neighboring farm. We even see stray cows and horses wander through from time to time. Things like that really do add a lot of charm to what could be just an ordinary downtown.

"Our main street is being developed to promote all kinds of locally owned businesses. But in addition to those, we have new churches, doctors' offices, schools, and housing developments. Our downtown is attractive and vibrant and was planned to look as good as it functions. And all of it is within walking distance of ample on-street parking. In this type of growth environment, having a sound and aggressive bank is in great demand because of the increased desire and need for new mortgages, business loans, and automobile loans." Cain paused before emphasizing, "My bank is perfectly positioned to be the bank that can meet all those needs. We are the oldest and biggest bank in the entire area, and now we have the new bank building to take us into the next century.

"There is huge potential for us to grow and expand our financial investment section. We just need to find the right people to help us get the word out. That is why this internship program is so important to us. If we can't find the perfect person, we are going to train them ourselves."

Will was listening intently and liked what he was hearing about this world that was so different than the one he was used to. "Gordon, that all sounds incredible."

Cain finally blurted out, "Why don't you just come work with me? You'd be great." He knew Will was perfect and exactly what they were looking for. Cain had seen plenty of evidence that Will was not afraid to approach and talk with anyone, was capable of bringing a lot of new business to the bank, and most importantly, could do it quickly.

Cain envisioned Will becoming the new face of GNB, and during the last week of classes, he repeatedly told him that after graduation he wanted him to come to Grayslake and meet the bank president.

CHAPTER 9

The Graduation

1957

Will and Cain accumulated enough credits to successfully graduate from the program. The graduation ceremony, held in the huge auditorium, was attended by hundreds of family members, colleagues, and friends, all of whom wanted to witness their graduates receive their prestigious certificates, and that included Carol and her parents. Will stood in the aisle, scanning the crowd for Cain. He wanted to finally introduce him to Carol and her folks, but Cain felt anxious and had retreated to the back row, where Will and Carol found him sitting alone.

Will said, "Gordon Cain, this is my wife, Carol."

Carol added, "It's very nice to meet you, Gordon. Will has told me so much about you."

Will asked, "Do you have family coming?"

Cain answered, "No, I didn't tell them about this."

Will and Carol said almost in tandem, "Then please come join us."

Cain smiled and nodded.

Will and Carol walked hand in hand down the long auditorium aisle. Cain followed and began to see how all the hours of conversations with Will were beginning to manifest in real life. He started to put faces to the names that he had heard so much about over the last ten weeks and saw how Will incorporated his feelings and actions into everyday life. When they arrived at their row of seats, Will introduced Cain to Carol's parents, "Gordon Cain, this is my mother-in-law, Sally Coates, and my father-in-law, Paul Coates."

Cain shook both of their hands. "It's nice to meet you both." Before sitting down next to Will, Cain looked to his left and noticed that Paul lifted the pleats of his pants before he sat down. Cain smiled as he thought to himself that it made sense to him now.

Will had been studying and trying to emulate his father-in-law who evidently was quite successful.

Cain was amazed at just how comfortable he felt with these people whom he had just met but quickly realized he had gotten to know them quite well over the last ten weeks. What did surprise him, though, was just how welcoming this family was to someone they had just met.

Cain reflected quietly and thought, maybe he was the lucky one. Perhaps Will would become more of an important friend than a coworker, someone to help him achieve his goals in this scheme. As Cain's name was read aloud, he started to make his way down the aisle toward the stage and could hear applause coming from the row he just vacated. This certificate really didn't mean anything to him professionally, but he found himself enjoying the moment and glanced back to see Will and Carol standing, clapping, and smiling at him. When he returned to his seat, Will, Carol, and her parents leaned toward him and quietly said, "Congratulations." Cain enjoyed this feeling as it had been a long time since he felt this level of closeness and acceptance.

A short time later, Will's name was read out, and Carol jumped to her feet as if she were sitting on a spring to applaud. She was so proud of his accomplishment and recognized how hard he had worked to achieve this certificate. Paul leaned over to Cain and whispered, "This is Will's third banking certificate. We think he has a very bright future, and we are very proud of him."

After the ceremony, graduates and their families gathered on the lawn, and Cain was surprised to see so many of the graduates coming over to Will to congratulate him and wish him luck. Will had obviously made an impression on his classmates and was well-liked.

Will knew each of them by name and introduced them to Carol, and for many, he even added some small anecdote of what he had learned about them over the last ten weeks. Cain stood astonished and just could not figure out when and how Will had managed to interact with all these people.

CHAPTER 10

The Brass Ring

1957

Will and Carol were back home at her parents' house in Villa Park. An exhausted Will was finally able to get some sleep in a comfortable bed but still woke early to get ready for his meeting in Grayslake. Carol, also up early, had pressed Will's best suit and dress shirt for him before helping her mother with breakfast. Once Will was dressed, he joined Carol and her parents for breakfast. Paul asked him in a somewhat teasing tone, "You think that old '46 will make it all the way up to Grayslake and back?"

Will replied with a chuckle and a grin, "Gee, I sure hope so. This would be the worst day for it to quit on me."

"You want to just take my car today?" offered Paul. "It's supposed to be a nice day. You can put the top down. I can drive the Fleetline today if you want me to."

Will replied, "Paul, that would be great... Thank you so much for offering. I'll make sure I fill the gas tank on my way back into town. I'm not sure how long this meeting will last, but I should be back before you all get home for lunch." Will left Carol with a kiss as he headed out the back door, and on his way to the garage, he heard Carol yell out from the screen porch, "Good luck! I love you!"

Will made the long drive to Grayslake and glanced down periodically at the directions Cain had written for him. He would nervously repeat the directions under his breath as he tried to not miss any turns that would cause him to be late. Will knew that this meeting was important and that if it went well, it could change the direction of his life.

He arrived with a few minutes to spare and decided to walk down the street to familiarize himself with the layout of the town and see what types of businesses were nearby. He thought that he could use that information to talk intelligently during his interview.

Grayslake National Bank was a huge building in the center of downtown that took up nearly an entire block. With an ornate brick-and-limestone façade, it reminded Will of his old high school in Lasalle. But now, the insecurity he felt as a seventeen-year-old was replaced by quiet confidence as he walked into this meeting.

Will was met by Cain at the front reception counter who smiled and said, "You made it. How was the drive up?"

Will answered, "Hi, Gordon, your directions were perfect. It was an easy drive." They shook hands as Cain said, "Follow me" and led Will on the long walk to the bank president's office.

During the walk, Will looked around and saw that the bank interior was spacious, clean, uncluttered, and very minimalistic. In contrast with the exterior, the interior had touches of modern glass and lighting paired with more traditional mahogany desks set throughout rooms with polished marble floors. Will found the interior just as impressive as the exterior. Cain knocked on the office door and heard "Come in" from the other side.

The president's office was the opposite of the lobby, with ornately beautiful mahogany wood panels that adorned each wall. The large desk and conference table were polished to a high gloss. And brown leather chairs were all set on plush, burgundy-colored carpeting. It was a very impressive room and provided a much warmer feeling than the lobby. Shaw said, "You must be Will. I'm Allen Shaw. Gordon has told me a lot of very good things about you. Thank you for making the trip up to meet with us this morning."

Shaw motioned for both men to sit at the conference table. Cain sat first, and Will sat next to him. Shaw walked to the opposite side, but before he sat, asked, "Will, would you like a coffee or a cold drink?"

Will politely declined, and Shaw said, "Will, Gordon and I have been talking quite a bit about you. We are very impressed with who you are, and we think that you would be a perfect fit for the growth program we have in mind here in Grayslake." Cain nodded in agreement with every word from Shaw.

Shaw laid out a couple of pieces of paper on the table in front of Will. He pointed at the first page and said, "We are creating a new position called client development manager with you specifically in mind. Your responsibilities will include being active and visible in the community as a representative of GNB. We want you to introduce the bank and our products to new clients and find creative ways for our existing customers to increase their presence at the bank. Will, you would also be providing leads to Gordon that he can use to grow the financial and investment sections."

Shaw slid the next page over and asked, "Any questions so far?"

Will responded, "No sir, not yet."

The Brass Ring

Shaw pointed at the second page and said, "Your compensation package would include this starting salary." He pointed at each line as he worked his way down the list. "In addition to that you would be included in our health insurance plan, which also includes a new vision plan that we just started. Preapproved bank financing for a new car. An expedited mortgage process to help you purchase a new home here in town. And lastly, here, an allowance to cover any incidental moving expenses you might have in making the move up here."

Shaw leaned back from the table. "Will, your desk will be positioned near the front door of the bank so you will have full visibility to all customers who enter the bank. And it is our expectation that you would engage with as many of our current customers as you can, in addition to bringing new customers into the bank."

Will tried to not let too much of his eagerness and excitement show through, but a big smile snuck out as Shaw again asked, "Will, do you have any questions?"

Will answered, "This is a lot to absorb, but I don't think I have any questions right now."

Shaw walked around the table, extended his hand to Will, and said, "Will, we want you here with us, and I think this offer expresses that desire. Please take some time to consider it. Discuss it with Carol and let us know what you think. We would very much like to get this program started as quickly as we can, but in the interim, if you have questions or think of anything we missed, please let us know and we'll address it."

Will shook Shaw's hand and offered a sincere, "Thank you, Mr. Shaw. I really appreciate you taking the time to meet with me and for extending this very generous offer."

Cain put his hand on Will's shoulder and said, "Will, you're going to be perfect for this. C'mon, I'll walk you out."

On the drive home, Will could not believe this was happening and drove with the top down, the radio on, sunshine beating on his face, and wind blowing through his hair. He thought, *Is all of this too good to be true?* He even began to doubt himself. *Can I actually do this job?*

It was no surprise that Will had blinders on when it came to this generous offer. He had dreamed of such an opportunity since he was a child. Now that he saw this brass ring within reach, he was going to grab it. No matter what.

He knew that Carol believed in him and that she knew he could do this. He also knew that Cain and Shaw would not have made this offer if they didn't think he could too. That was enough to reassure and convince him that he could not pass this up.

Will arrived home, took the papers from GNB, and laid them out on the dining room table. He sat quietly at the table, looked at each page, and rehearsed what Shaw had said to him earlier. When he heard a car door close in the driveway, he ran to the doorway and yelled out through the screen door, "Hurry, I have news."

Carol and her parents sat together on one side of the dining room table as Will played the part of Shaw from the opposite side and reviewed every detail of GNB's offer. Carol couldn't hold it in any longer; she screamed out in excitement, hopped up from her seat, and wrapped her arms around Will's neck to give him a big kiss.

Will had just one recurring concern with the timing of all this. He thought about the relationships, loyalty, and respect he had for his fellow workers at Ottawa National Bank. He had convinced them to pay his tuition for the class in Madison because they would benefit from his attendance in the program.

Will went to President Hoffman that afternoon and said, "Good afternoon, sir, do you have a minute for me?"

Hoffman, a career banker, had been the president of ONB for over twenty years.

Unlike Shaw, who was still relatively new to his position, Hoffman had experienced every facet of financial transactions, regulations, and principles. He was a consummate professional and took great pride in understanding the financial markets and the responsibility of managing his clients. He also took great pride in his appearance and his work ethic.

His short gray hair was kept neatly combed and parted on the side, and he was always in a suit, dress shirt, and necktie. Hoffman was clearly busy as he looked up over the top of his glasses, but he waved Will in and asked, "Will, what's on your mind?" as he continued to shuffle papers around his desk.

Will answered, "Mr. Hoffman, this is a very difficult thing for me to say, but I'm here to let you know that I'm leaving the bank. I need to give you my two weeks' notice."

Will now had Hoffman's full attention as he stopped what he was doing, took off his glasses, and asked, "Why?"

"This morning, I drove up to Grayslake for a meeting with the president of Grayslake National Bank. They have offered me a management job in a newly created area called client development, and it's a great opportunity for me. I feel terrible about having to leave ONB, but this opportunity is perfectly suited for me."

Hoffman had seen everything there was to see in banking and seemed skeptical as he heard that. He asked, "Will, are you sure about this? What is client development?"

Will responded confidently, "I will be overseeing the growth of clients and bringing new business into the bank. It's a salaried, management position, and they believe I can do it."

Hoffman replied, "That sounds more like an outside sales position than a banking job. Are you sure you want to leave banking to do sales work? And how many new accounts do you need to generate to make any money?"

Will answered, "They are offering me a lot of money and will help me with a mortgage, a new car loan, and moving expenses to get me up there. It's an opportunity that I just can't pass up. My starting salary will be more than my father ever made in his life.

"I watched my father struggle without money all my life. I have to do this. I trust them." Then Will said, "The difficult part for me is that you have been very good to me. You gave me a chance to show what I could do here, and I am grateful for every opportunity you have given. It's also important to me that I leave you the right way and on good terms. So, to help with that, I'd like to ask you to allow me to reimburse the full cost of my tuition for the Madison program before I leave."

Hoffman was fond of Will, and although he had his doubts about this offer, he did recognize that this was something that Ottawa National Bank could not match.

So, Hoffman said, "Will, I think your willingness to repay the bank for your tuition shows extraordinary character, and I appreciate you making the offer. I agree that it is the right thing to do."

Hoffman retrieved Will's personnel file from the drawer and handed him a copy of the receipt. Will realized that he did not have that much money saved and asked, "Would it be okay with you if I repaid this on my last day?"

Hoffman replied, "Of course."

Before Will left the office, Hoffman said, "Will, I think you'll be great in your new job. They're lucky to have you. Good luck."

Now that Will had committed to Grayslake, he and Carol were excited that their first home was now within reach and were anxious to start looking.

But they decided that rather than move more than needed, Will would commute to start, and they would continue to live at Carol's parents' house until they found their new home in Grayslake.

Before they could start to look at houses, however, Will needed to find the money to repay Ottawa National Bank. So, Carol suggested that they ask her father for a loan.

That evening they approached Paul as he sat in his favorite chair in the living room. He was watching the news and snacking on cocktail peanuts as Carol asked, "Daddy, can we talk to you a minute?"

Paul answered, "Sure, honey, what is it?"

Will interjected, "Paul, I accepted the job in Grayslake today after I met with Hoffman to give my two weeks' notice. I told Hoffman that I wanted to repay the cost of my Madison tuition before I left, but we don't have enough saved right now to do that."

Then Carol said, "Dad, we were hoping that maybe you could help lend us the money to pay that back." She very quickly added, "We'll pay you back as quick as we can, we promise."

Paul replied, "Of course I can help you with that."

Carol said, "Thank you, Daddy."

Will added, "Thanks, Paul," but as he shook his hand, Paul added, "I'll loan you the money, but it will need to draw the same amount of interest that I would receive from my bank."

The following morning, Will spoke with Cain on the phone and shared the idea of him commuting to start and said, "Carol and I are excited to start looking for a home up there, but we thought that rather than move more than we need to, I would just commute back and forth to start."

Cain responded, "Okay, that's not a problem. You can do that."

Will added, "All I have is this old 1946 Chevy that I drove to school in Madison, and I'm worried that it might not be reliable enough to make the trip to Grayslake and back every day. I think I may need to get something to make the commute easier and more reliable."

Cain asked, "You want to buy a new car?"

Will replied, "I think I do. Can the bank help me with that?"

"Of course. Let's do an application right now over the phone."

Cain called a couple of days later and told him, "You're approved for up to $3,000, so go shopping. You can come up here if you want. I know a guy at the Chevy dealer. He can help you."

CHAPTER 11

The Bel Air

1957

Will's big day finally arrived, and in keeping with the current, long stretch of beautiful summer weather that town was enjoying, it was another clear and warm August day as Will set out to purchase his very first new car. He was filled with excitement as he made the drive north to Grayslake in what might be his last ride in his 1946 Chevrolet Fleetline. He had driven this old car thousands of miles, but today he seemed to notice more than ever before every creak, rattle, and thud his old car made during every bump and turn along the way.

On the drive north, Will thought exclusively about new cars and how he had always been fond of the Chevrolet Bel Air. He thought the car looked great, the name sounded classy, and he knew it was popular among people in his age group. In a word, the Bel Air was "cool," and Will wanted one. The old '46 Chevy made one last loud clunk as the front tires rolled over the curb on its way into the dealership parking lot. Will parked near the front door and walked directly to a long line of brand-new Bel Air coupes parked out front.

Will was drawn to one in larkspur blue and thought it the perfect color. It was one of the last of the 1957s they had in stock and even had the optional white top and white interior that he wanted so badly. And because it was one of the last 1957s, he also thought that it might be a little cheaper than the new 1958s already hitting the lot. This '57 also included air-conditioning and an automatic transmission, both options that Will would normally choose to live without, but this car represented the new life he was starting, and he would take all the options. This was an easy sale as Cain's friend helped to complete all the paperwork before he handed Will the keys to his brand-new Bel Air.

Will took a few minutes and allowed himself to settle comfortably into the smooth vinyl plushness of the driver's seat as he turned the key over and heard the low roar of the modern fuel-injected V8 engine. He looked at each of the gauges on the futuristic dashboard, made his seat adjustments, and repositioned the mirrors to his liking. Then he grabbed the chromed column shifter and dropped the automatic transmission into drive. The car rolled forward toward the exit before Will paused to give one last, long look at his old, black '46 Fleetline now parked in the used car line.

It was his first car and had been very good to him. Will sat quietly and stared at his old friend, smiling as memories flashed through his mind. The Friday nights at the drive-in, learning to drive on the long dirt roads at the farm, and Carol's feet, her toenails painted bright red, doing dance steps up on the dash during the long drive to California. While reminiscing, he realized that he had underestimated just how much he loved that old car and how attached he was to it. Finally, he slid the transmission into reverse and backed up to the dealership door.

Will walked back over to his old friend and stood for just a minute or two as his hand rested on the warm black paint of the hood before he slid his hand over some small scratches on the fender, caused by the car rolling down the hill and into some bushes when he forgot to set the parking brake up at the old tree. That memory made him smile and convinced him to walk back into the dealership. He went directly to the salesman's desk and told him that he had changed his mind.

The salesman initially looked worried as he thought that this new car deal was falling apart, but then looked relieved when Will continued, "I'm going to keep my old car rather than trade it in. Is it too late to do that?"

The salesman answered, "That shouldn't be a problem, Will. Give me a couple of minutes to make the changes." The salesman adjusted the paperwork and found that Will was still under the $3,000 he was approved for. So, Will asked him, "Can you just hold on to my '46 for me? I'll be back tomorrow morning to pick it up with my younger brother. So, when you see him with me, toss him the keys. It's going to be his first car now."

Will made the long, and now much smoother and quieter, drive home from the dealership with his windows down, the radio on, and his left arm out the window. With the warm sunshine beating down on him, he was reminded of the drive home after his initial interview in Grayslake while driving Paul's Sunliner. But this time, it was his brand-new car. Will knew that he was the first in his family to own a new car, something his father always wanted but never achieved. This was a feeling that Will had never experienced before, and he was feeling good about himself and was excited at the prospect of many more days like this.

CHAPTER 12

The First Day

1957

It was Monday, August 26, 1957, an important date for Will. He was awake at 5:30 a.m., after a restless night of nervous excitement, and got up to shower, shave, and spend a few extra minutes in the mirror to make sure he looked his best. And why shouldn't he? Everything had led to this moment. He was certain that today would be the beginning of the life he and Carol had always dreamed of.

He grabbed his best suit from the closet as Carol walked into the bedroom, and without a word, gave him a kiss. She was hiding a small box behind her back and offered a warm smile as she brought the box around in her right hand. Her eyes were bright with excitement and pride for him as he took the box, untied the ribbon, and opened it to find the new necktie she had picked out especially for this first day. Also included was a new tie clip. A simple and plain, polished, sterling silver bar that Will turned over. His eyes began to well up as he saw that on the back, Carol had inscribed the word "Proud." Will looked at Carol and saw tears running down her face as well as she watched him open her gift.

Will put on his new tie and tied the perfect Windsor knot as Carol sat on the edge of the bed watching him and telling him how nice he looked. Will straightened his tie in the mirror and then strategically placed the tie clip in the perfect location before he extended his hand to Carol to pull her to her feet. He wrapped his arms around her waist, pulled her close, and said, "I love you so much. Thank you for this and for believing in us. I won't let you down."

Sally had prepared a nice breakfast so the entire family could eat together before Will needed to get out the door and on the road. But before he could leave, Paul and Sally presented him with another gift.

It was a new, black leather briefcase. They stood together as Paul said, "If you're going into business, you'll need one of these."

Will said, "Thank you" to both Paul and Sally and patted Henry on the head as he walked toward the door. There was no way he was going to allow himself to be late on his first day.

Will arrived in Grayslake and found his desk just inside the front door. He placed his briefcase on the desk as he eased himself into his new high-back leather chair and found that the desk had been fully stocked with pencils, pens, and a personalized notepad that read "From the desk of Will Hays." The top page of the notepad had a handwritten note from Shaw: "Congratulations, Will, and welcome to GNB. We're happy to have you here with us." Will also noticed that his desk calendar already had two entries. The first for today: "Lunch with Gordon at noon." The second was on Tuesday: "Weekly Staff Meeting 10 a.m."

An attractive woman walked over to his desk and introduced herself, "Good morning, Mr. Hays, I'm Donna Carlisle, and I am the head teller here. Mr. Shaw asked me to show you around the bank and introduce you to the rest of the staff and department heads." The remainder of the morning was filled with introductions and a walking tour of the bank and additional offices on the second floor.

At about 11:45 a.m., Cain made his way to Will's desk. "I'll bet you've had a busy morning, but I have something for you." Cain handed Will a box with a small bow taped to the top. Will opened the box and saw a dark-brown mahogany desk nameplate that had "Will Hays" engraved in gold letters. Cain was never comfortable with sentiment, so he quickly defaulted and said, "You ready for lunch?" They made the short walk down the street to the local diner.

Will, preoccupied with looking around at the downtown buildings and businesses, was completely unaware of passing vehicle traffic, but Cain noticed the dark green Ford Fairlane that drove by slowly, headed toward the bank. It was occupied by La Monica's guys, and they were carrying the first drop of "Outfit" money to Shaw. Cain felt a renewed sense of urgency to get this plan going, so they used their time at lunch to start collaborating on a strategy.

They sat at a booth along the window. Cain jumped right in and said, "First, the Chamber of Commerce. You'll need to join that right away and then get a complete list of all the businesses in town. They update that list frequently, so stay on top of that." Will pulled a small notepad from his jacket pocket and started taking notes. Cain continued, "You and Carol should join a church up here. Church may offer some ways to reach people that do not live or work in Grayslake." Will looked up quickly from writing and said, "Okay." Cain went right back to it. "Lions Club, Jaycees, you get the idea." Cain paused for a sip of water, then added, "Start working your way through town going door to door if you have to. We need to get this going right away."

CHAPTER 13

The Home of Their Own

1958

Will had been making his daily walks through town for about five months now, and on this cold January morning, he prepared for the day's frigid temperatures. Like a mailman, he would not be dissuaded from his responsibilities. He pulled on rubber galoshes over his black, leather wingtip shoes, wrapped a scarf around his neck, put on his black wool overcoat, and topped it off with a black, fur Cossack hat. As he walked outside, he was immediately hit in the face by arctic-cold wind and blowing snow. These daily walks had become routine for Will as he steadily got to know every business in town. Each time Will rang the bell as a business door swung open, store owners and employees had another chance to be amazed at the tenacity and drive that he exhibited as he brought the message of GNB to the community. Will spoke with confidence and charisma as he introduced the current and future banking programs that he thought would benefit both business owners and their employees. Will incorporated personal stories about himself and frequently asked questions about what was happening in the lives of those he pitched to, making each visit feel more like a conversation between friends than just a sterile sales call.

Will was on the move from morning to night, working through the list provided by the Chamber of Commerce. By then he had introduced himself to every business on the list, and for many, he was now on his second or sometimes third follow-up visit. He checked in with the chamber every week for any additions or changes.

Every time Cain or Shaw looked out their office windows, no matter the time or weather, they saw Will making his way up and down the sidewalks of Center Street. He constantly talked with anyone he encountered in town.

Will and Carol had also been attending St. Paul's Lutheran Church in nearby Round Lake for several months, making the long drive there every Sunday morning from Villa Park. Even at church, Will found ways to incorporate GNB into conversations with people before and after the services.

On the ride home from church one Sunday, Carol was annoyed with him and asked, "Do you have to talk about business even when we are at church? Can't you just take a break from that for an hour or two? I see people rolling their eyes and trying to avoid us because they are tired of hearing the same old thing from you every Sunday. We are not going to make any friends here if you don't stop with your persistent badgering."

Will, frustrated, barked back, "Badgering? Honey, this is a numbers game for me. The reason I'm out working so much is because I'm trying to talk to as many people as I can because I know that just a fraction of them will actually open a new account or move business to us.

"I come to church to profess my faith in God and thank Him for all the blessings He provides us. I am not there to make friends, and I am going to do whatever I can, and use whatever means I can, to give us the life that God wants us to have together." After saying that, Will saw how dejected and surprised Carol was by his response. So, he took a deep breath and spoke a bit softer. "Honey, I want you to be happy, and I do want you to enjoy church. And like you, I do want us to make friends here, so I will try to give it a rest while we are at church. Okay?"

Carol knew that all Will wanted was for her to be happy. And she knew how hard he was working and that he was doing all of it to build the life they wanted together, so she assured, "Thank you, honey. I love you and our life together."

By spring's arrival, Will had joined the Lions Club, Elks Club, and Jaycees and was even playing softball two nights a week with the Jaycees' men's league. Because he was the shortest guy on the team, his teammates gave him the nickname "Half-Pint" and had that name printed on the back of his jersey. Will was not crazy about the nickname, but it paled in comparison to what his brother used to call him. So, he made the best of it and embraced the fact that he felt like one of the guys. Will was taking all of this seriously and would give it his best effort in every way.

After several months, Will found that he really was left alone to manage his work and implement his ideas. At weekly staff meetings he provided updates on his progress and demonstrated metrics that clearly indicated that new accounts were on the rise.

Cain added that he was also seeing a marked increase in investment dollars as well. And although it had been just a few months, Shaw and Cain were very pleased with Will's work so far.

Will reached out to Cain to let him know that he and Carol wanted to spend more time attending church activities, and that included joining the choir. That would mean more trips for Carol on weeknights, and with him using their only car to commute to work, it would not be possible for her to do that. So, Will asked Cain what it would take for them to start the search for a home in Grayslake. Cain told Will that a new housing subdivision had just begun construction very close to the lake and just a few blocks from downtown.

Cain said that a lot of young families were buying lots and building homes there and that many of those families were professionals. Cain told Will that could mean a tremendous upside for instant equity in that area.

THE FOLLOWING SUNDAY AFTER CHURCH, WILL AND Carol drove slowly through town exploring what would become their new hometown. They looked at each building as if it were their first time truly seeing it. The Bel Air turned the corners slowly as it wound through town and into the new subdivision that Cain had described to them. The car climbed a slight hill, and as the road crested, Will stopped to look through the windshield at the beautiful blue water of Gray's Lake below. Except for this new road carved in along the west side, the lake was surrounded by rolling hills of freshly planted cornfields.

Will took his foot off the brake and allowed the car to slowly roll downhill. At the bottom, they found that construction was underway on a new community center. The artist's rendering on the sign showed a sleek and modern building and described seasonal summer camp and swimming programs for children, along with ice skating and sledding in winter months. It would also house a preschool program for the community's residents. That intersection had a new green street sign installed with "HARVEY AVE" printed in bright white letters. Carol grinned as she told Will, "This is probably a sign. My mother's maiden name is Harvey."

Several houses along that street had been started, and as they reached the top of the next hill, Will pulled over to the right curb and stopped again. They both got out of the car and looked back at the lake from their vantage point. It truly was beautiful. Will took Carol by the hand as they looked at the plywood marker staked in the center of the lot next to them with "413" on it in black spray paint. Will told Carol, "Maybe this is another sign? Philippians 4:13 is one of my favorite bible passages. 'I can do all things through Christ who strengthens me.'" They held each other's hand and walked to the center of that lot, where Carol said, "This could be our new front yard."

Will turned to Carol and asked, "Is it?"

Carol smiled while throwing her arms around Will's neck and whispered, "I think it is. I think we're home."

Over the next couple of days, Will did a little more research and found that lot 413 had nice woods with full mature trees right behind it and that those woods backed up to property owned by the local school district. He also learned that the school district planned to construct a new elementary school on the southern portion of their property and that their initial plan was to leave the northern end wooded and untouched. That would likely mean that Will and Carol's backyard would not be overlooked by any neighboring homes, and the back of the house would have a beautiful, wooded view. A new school within walking distance would also be beneficial if they were to start a family and would certainly increase their property value as well.

With that information in hand, Will told Cain, "We found a beautiful lot on Harvey Avenue, and we think we want to build a house on it. Can you tell me what we need to do next?"

"Great," said Cain. "Let's do a mortgage application, and we'll get the process started." Will completed a mortgage application, and a few weeks later, got an approval for $15,000.

That was enough to cover the cost of the lot and the construction of the house. Will and Carol closed on their first mortgage a couple of months later.

As first-time homebuyers, Will and Carol were filled with excitement but moved somewhat conservatively and found a Sears house to build. The Sears new home kits were growing in popularity at that time because they came complete with plans, materials, and a builder to build the house. They decided on a cute little ranch house for just under $13,000. It would be a combination of brick and siding with two bedrooms, one bathroom, an attached one-car garage, and a full basement. They added a third bedroom to the plan because they were thinking ahead to the possibility of children. Will recognized that the idea of buying a lot, building a house, and other unexpected costs associated with new house construction would mean that repaying Paul for the tuition loan would need to be delayed a while longer.

Will spoke with Paul that evening and explained that with this new house build, he would need more time to get him repaid. Paul saw Will's hard work and understood that he was doing all he could to give Carol the life she wanted and deserved. Paul told him to take as much time as he needed and not to worry about it but reminded him that the interest would continue to accrue until the loan was paid in full.

Construction on their new home began in the fall, and Will and Carol made frequent visits to the build site. First to see the foundation, then the framing, and then every other step along the way.

As each step started, they would imagine what the house would look like when completed and would spend countless hours walking imaginary hallways and rooms. Carol spent giddy moments fantasizing about every aspect of her new kitchen and would stand at her imaginary sink looking out what would be a window at the woods in her backyard.

Each visit was documented with a picture or two so Carol could share the progress with her parents and friends. They each took turns posing proudly as the other would snap a picture or two on the Polaroid camera. Will and Carol waited patiently as construction moved slower than they expected but were overjoyed when the house was finally completed the following spring.

CHAPTER 14

The Governor

1959

Will and Carol stood hand in hand on the front porch of their new home as they watched delivery men moving a new sofa through the front door. They looked at each other and thought, *Could this all be real?* A new home, a new car in the driveway, and now new furniture being delivered inside. There would be no more hand-me-downs, garage sales, or thrift stores. They believed they were going to make it and were well on their way to reaching the American dream.

Will was a visible fixture on the streets of Grayslake and continued to bring new business to the bank. He was rapidly developing a strong reputation among town residents and business owners as being friendly, knowledgeable, trustworthy, and honest. As a member in good standing of the Chamber of Commerce, the chamber's board of directors asked Will if he would be interested in running for the position of secretary, which would soon be vacated. Will was elected and would be participating in monthly meetings and contributing his voice to the direction the Chamber of Commerce would take in future years.

It was just about eighteen months since Will joined GNB, and Cain and Shaw called him in for an evaluation conference to let him know just how much they appreciated the work he was doing. Individual and business accounts had increased by more than 50 percent, and the investment banking section had grown by nearly 23 percent during that same time period. That was when Cain asked Will for the first time, "Are you ready to invest some of your money with me?" Cain showed him some of the returns he had been making lately and said, "You could pay off your car loan in just a few months."

Will remembered that he still needed to repay Paul for his school tuition loan and thought it would be nice if he could get that paid off sooner rather than later. Cain told him, "You probably have some equity in the house already." And Cain suggested that he take out a second mortgage on the house and use that money to invest with him.

Cain told him, "A $5,000 investment today could yield a return of as much as $8,000 in just a few months." Will applied for a second mortgage on the house and Cain was right in that he did have some equity in the house already. The second mortgage was approved a short time later, and Will gave Cain $5,000 to invest. After about six months, Cain called him into his office and with a big smile said, "I told you!" as he handed Will a check for $7,980.

That was enough to repay the second mortgage, along with some savings Will could use to repay Paul, with interest. Will was impressed with Cain and now integrated this personal investment success story with prospective bank clients and others looking to invest their money with Cain.

With a check in hand to repay the loan, Will and Carol called her parents and made a date to meet for dinner. Her mother suggested cooking at home rather than going out, so they all agreed to meet at Paul and Sally's house that Friday evening. Will and Carol arrived and saw Sally sitting at the piano while Paul and Henry stood together playing their violins. Will and Carol smiled at each other and walked over to sing along. Once the impromptu concert was completed, they all sat together before dinner, and Will thanked Paul for all his help and especially his patience as he handed Paul the check. The loan was now repaid in full, and Paul generously told them that he was always there to help them if needed.

LIVINGSTON WALKED CONFIDENTLY ALONE DOWN A LONG corridor of polished marble in the Illinois State Capital. His hair was combed neatly, and he wore a dark brown three-piece suit, along with his trademark, matching monochromatic plaid vest. He arrived at a large, arched mahogany door that had a placard next to it that read, "Governor's Office, Honorable William G. Stratton."

Livingston pushed open the door and was met by the governor's secretary seated at her desk in the outer office. She greeted Livingston. "Good morning, Mr. Livingston, the governor is expecting you. You can go right in." As Livingston moved to the governor's office door, she added, "Can I bring you a cup of coffee or tea?"

Livingston looked back, offered a warm smile, and said, "Nothing for me, thank you." He entered the office and saw that the governor was with a man he did not recognize. Governor Stratton stood from his desk. He was tall and proportionally thick, which made for an imposing figure. If he had been shorter, he might have given the impression that he was overweight, but he carried his girth well on his large frame. His appearance was also distinguished and stately as he wore a gray suit with a thin tie. His dark hair was oiled and slicked straight back, resembling the kind of hairstyle one might see in an old gangster movie. His clean-shaven face made him appear much younger than his fifty-nine years. Stratton served in the Navy and worked in Chicago as a lawyer before being elected to the U.S. House of Representatives. He was well-educated and articulate, and his deep voice still had that obvious Chicago accent as he greeted Livingston by saying, "Sam Livingston, thanks for making the trip down to meet with me."

Livingston replied, "It's an honor, governor. Thank you for the invitation."

Stratton introduced the other man in the office, "Sam, this is Robert Thomas. Bob is the chairman of the Republican party here in Illinois." Stratton told Thomas, "Sam here is Charles Livingston's son."

Livingston asked, "Oh, you know my father?"

Stratton replied, "Sam, your father and I have known each other a long time. I had a shingle out on your dad's beat many years ago, and the last time I saw him was at Dailey's inauguration last year. Is he still in Bridgeport?"

Livingston replied, "Yes, he's still at the '9,' but he's been thinking more and more about retiring since they passed him up on another promotion. I suspect he'll stick around for another year or maybe two."

Stratton asked Livingston, "What happened? He didn't want you to work with him?"

Livingston answered, "Well, he wanted me in the law, but he didn't want me walking the beat like he did. And he really didn't want his son to need to be on the take to get ahead in the department. So, he decided that law school would be a better way for me to fight crime. And he was right, as usual."

Stratton agreed, "Fathers usually are." He suddenly changed the subject. "Now that we have all the formal bullshit out of the way, let me tell you why you are here. As you may already know, I am seeking a third term, and it is starting to look like this is going to be a very close race with Kerner. When I saw your father, he told me about your work going after La Monica and the Outfit. I've been thinking quite a bit about what your dad told me, and I admire your persistence. I did some checking and I'm impressed with what I've seen from you so far. You are doing some good things up there."

Livingston said, "Well, governor, that's awfully kind of you to say that, but I'm not convinced it's been that successful of late. We have been tracking plenty of leads and trying to generate information, but most have led to dead ends, and it is becoming more apparent that the Outfit has moved its money out of Cook County. So, we are at a bit of a dead end on what our office can do."

Stratton interjected, "Don't be too hard on yourself. The way I see it, the problem you're having is that you are trying to follow money that you can't see. The agencies that you need to help you, like the Federal Reserve Bank and the Department of Justice, will not work directly with county prosecutors. They prefer to work at the state level with a state attorney general." Livingston's face showed excitement, apprehension, and some nervousness at what the governor might be suggesting.

Stratton continued, "I know that you are probably starting to think about a second term up there, but I was hoping that we could talk about how you see your future in this state." Stratton paused, looked straight into Livingston's eyes, and said, "I would like you to consider being the attorney general for the great state of Illinois. Then you can go after the mob with the full weight of the state behind you. Having you run for attorney general on our ticket could help both of us in this next election cycle. Getting La Monica locked up would be a great feather in your cap as well, and who knows, maybe you'll want to run for governor when I'm done."

Stratton was all business and moved quickly to try to close this deal. He extended his hand to Livingston. "So, do we have a deal, or do you need some time to think about it?"

Livingston reflected briefly and looked over at Thomas who was nodding in hopeful anticipation.

Livingston admired Stratton and the directness he exhibited, and he desperately wanted to continue his pursuit of La Monica and the mob. So, he stood and took Stratton's hand. "We have a deal. I can be available to start campaigning whenever you need me."

Stratton replied, "Great news, Sam. I'm looking forward to working with you."

Livingston responded, "Thank you, governor. I appreciate the confidence you have in me, and I'll work as hard as I can for the people of Illinois."

Stratton answered, "I know you will, Sam. That's why you're here."

Livingston shook Thomas' hand as well and said, "And thank you, Mr. Thomas. I look forward to working with you as well."

CHAPTER 15

The Dinner

1960

Will and Carol had furnished and decorated their new home and were now completely settled and standing firmly on their own. They were both planners by nature and had always talked about their goals and how to achieve them. On this cold Friday evening in January, snow had just begun to fall as Will pulled into the driveway after a long week of work. He gathered his belongings from the car before he walked through the light dusting of snow on the front walk toward the front door.

Carol had been planning this evening for several days. She went out that afternoon to buy a new dress and stopped at the salon to get her hair and makeup done. She stood at the front door and waited to greet him in her new blue dress and matching high-heeled shoes. She had her hair up in a modified beehive hairdo that she saw her favorite actress wear in a magazine photo. She accessorized her new dress with her favorite pearl necklace, bracelet, and earrings that Will had given her for Christmas. Carol's maturity and beauty were now on full display, and she had grown into an extraordinarily beautiful woman.

Will dropped his briefcase and coat as Carol wrapped her arms around his neck and kissed him hello. Will looked around to see that the dining room table was set for a nice dinner and that Carol had candles lit on the table and around the living room. Will leaned back to look at her and said, "You look gorgeous. What's the occasion?"

Carol smiled and said, "I just thought it would be nice to sit and eat a nice meal together while we talk about something I've had on my mind lately."

They sat at the table as Will said, "This looks delicious. Thank you, honey. What's on your mind?"

Carol smiled warmly and said, "I'm home here alone all day while you are working, and I thought it might be a good time for us to talk about having a baby and growing our family."

Will's face showed surprise, but he just sat quietly. His silence made Carol nervous and then even a bit upset. "What is it?" she asked. "I thought you would be happy."

Will looked down and put his hand on his forehead before he looked up at Carol, and with a tear in his eye, said, "I don't think my father ever loved me. He certainly never told me he did. What if I don't know how to be a good dad?"

Carol got up, walked around behind Will, put her arms around his neck, and whispered quietly in his ear, "Just do everything for our kids that you wish your dad had done for you. And someday when our kids grow up and want to have kids of their own, they won't need to ask that same question. Let's just love our kids as much as we love each other, and everything will work out fine."

After dinner, Will put on some soft music and asked Carol to dance with him. A neighbor who was out walking his dog as snow accumulated in the street stopped in his tracks and watched the two lovebirds through the picture window as they danced in the candlelight. Will held Carol tightly with his hands around her waist, and Carol had her arms around his neck as they danced slowly cheek to cheek. The neighbor stood in the kind of quiet that could only be provided by freshly fallen snow and thought to himself that it looked like the kind of romantic scene one might see in a snow globe.

Months went by with no success in getting pregnant, and on the advice of Carol's doctor, they both went through some initial fertility testing. Once the testing was completed, doctors shared the difficult news with them that they were unable to have children.

Carol took the news badly, but Will was always there to love and comfort her, and he introduced the idea of adoption.

For the next few weeks, they spent every moment together talking about the idea. Will and Cain had grown to be quite close, so Will shared this idea with Cain over lunch one day. Cain told him that one of his investment clients was a prominent adoption attorney in Waukegan, where all the county services departments were located. Will made the call, gave him a retainer, and was provided with all the initial paperwork. Over the next few weeks, Will, Carol, and each of their family members completed their portions of the forms.

Will submitted the forms for review, and another few months went by before a notice arrived that interview dates were scheduled. Will and Carol were now thoroughly vetted and found to be a viable adoption family. Then in early October, they were told by their attorney that a baby boy would be available soon. In early December, the baby was born, and the adoption process concluded four days later, when Will and Carol brought him home from the hospital. From that moment on, it seemed that their entire universe revolved around that little boy.

To say congratulations, GNB sent an elaborate gift basket of toys and clothing, and the happy news made its way through the entire community. At home on a Saturday afternoon, Carol stood in the hallway holding the baby and watched Will on the ladder as he gave the nursery a fresh coat of paint and hung some cute wallpaper. Time moved quickly and the baby was healthy, happy, and growing. And before long, first words and first steps were witnessed and shared with proud grandparents, friends, and neighbors.

IT WAS LATE ON A FRIDAY NIGHT, AND SHAW WAS SEATED at the conference table in his office with a large stack of manilla folders piled up in front of him. Cain walked into the office and said, "Allen, I stayed to make those late rotations, but I'm on my way home now. Everyone else is gone for the night. What are you doing here so late?"

Shaw didn't look up from his work as he answered, "Just doing some research."

Cain asked, "Do you have a minute to talk before I head out?"

Shaw looked up over the top of his glasses and responded, "Sure, come on in. What do you need?"

Cain walked over to the table. "What is all of this?"

Shaw replied, "Mortgage applications for every doctor and lawyer that has bought a house through us in the last two years."

Cain asked, "Why?"

"I'm looking at their average annual incomes and then comparing that to the average cost of the homes they purchased," answered Shaw.

"What do you need to do that for?"

Shaw replied, "Delores and I are looking to buy a bigger house. But I need it to fit into these same criteria. I want it to be nice and something that suits a bank president, but it can't be too flashy or over the top because I can't draw too much unwanted attention from you know who."

Cain said, "Well, that's actually what I wanted to talk to you about. Moving all this money around has become a lot more work than I think we both expected, and I feel like I'm the one doing most of the work and taking most of the risk in this. And if we get caught, this is all going to be hung on me. I haven't gotten any money out of this since you gave me that initial $10,000 when we started. And if I'm taking all this risk, then I need more money."

Shaw removed his glasses, leaned back in his chair, and in frustration said, "Gordon, listen to me. Lennox isn't dumping piles of money on my desk anymore. The money he did give me, I needed to share with you to get this whole thing started. I also had to give $15,000 to Barnes in Round Lake to get him involved and then another $15,000 to Joseph in Hainesville to get him going."

Cain sensed Shaw's frustration in his response, so he exuded a bit of his own and said, "Don't tell me you're not making money on this deal with the new suits and new car, and now you are shopping for a new house. I'm just asking for something more for all the work I'm doing."

Shaw stood, not to confront Cain but instead to look at him eye to eye. "Gordon, we're friends first and foremost, and we are in this together. But make no mistake, and let's not kid ourselves, if we get caught, we will definitely both go down for this. If I had more money to give you, I would, but I don't, so you'll just need to figure something else out."

Cain asked, "What if I already did?"

"Already did what?"

"Figured something else out."

Shaw slowly sat back in his chair, leaned back comfortably, and said, "So, this is what you came in to talk about." He smirked. "Let's hear it."

Cain leaned in and softly said, "I think I figured out a way to skim some small amounts of cash from drops that are coming in."

Shaw was quick to respond, "No, no, no…. No fucking way! We are not stealing from Lennox. That guy will fucking kill both of us."

Cain continued, "Allen, just listen. I think I can skim some off the top of the drops while it is still in the float and before it gets assigned into accounts. I tried it a couple of times this week, and when I ran the report today, I was able to make that cash disappear from the P&Ls. If I can do that, then I can keep it off the balance sheets. If anyone ever did question a discrepancy, it would look like the guys making the drops took the money rather than me. If I keep it as small amounts, I know I can keep it undetected."

Shaw's body language was defiant as he leaned back with his arms crossed as Cain continued, "You brought me into this to make money, and you need me to do this. But Allen, you're the only one of us making any money, and that's not right. I need to make all this effort and risk worthwhile for me too. I can do this, and I promise you, I won't get caught. It's just a few dollars here and there. No one will even miss it."

Shaw was listening carefully and was measured in his response. "If you do this, and for the record, I don't think you should, and you know who would get suspicious, is there a way for you to put money back in without anyone knowing it was gone?"

"I thought about that too. If I keep the amounts small, then I could adjust that amount back into the float and then disburse it back into accounts as usual. That way if anyone did an audit, all the money would be accounted for. No harm, no foul. It would just look like a clerical error. The only way Lennox would ever find out money was missing would be if he decided to pull all the money out at one time rather than do an audit, but I think it is unlikely that he would do that. So, what do you think?"

Shaw shook his head but then shrugged as he said, "I don't think you should, but if you are sure you won't get caught, then go ahead if you want. Just don't let any of this come back on me."

"Okay, thanks, Allen. I'll be careful. Trust me."

As Cain left the office, Shaw adjusted his glasses and went back to reviewing the files.

CHAPTER 16

The New Shaw

1961

Shaw made the now-familiar annual drive to Lake Forest, but this time, he drove his new 1961 Chevrolet Corvair coupe in bright red with the matching red interior. And this time, he drove noticeably slower on the gravel road to avoid throwing stones that could chip the paint. He slowed to a stop as he reached the gate and was approached by a new man at Baker's post. Shaw rolled down his window and asked, "Where is Mike Baker?"

The new man answered, "Baker is up at the main house now. Can I have your name?"

"I'm Allen Shaw and I am here to see Mr. La Monica and Mr. Lennox."

"They're expecting you." He signaled to open the gate.

Shaw parked in his usual spot next to Lennox, looked back at his new car, and felt a little better about himself. He walked to the front door and was greeted by the butler who said, "Good morning, Mr. Shaw. They are waiting for you in the office." Shaw walked down the long hallway toward the stairs with a new haircut, new and more modern wire-framed glasses, and his new, and tailored this time, blue pinstripe suit. He walked into the office, and Lennox immediately noticed and greeted Shaw. "A new car and now a new suit. And you finally got one that fits. Good for you, Allen. Or are you having a midlife crisis?"

La Monica was less impressed and got right down to business. "I don't give two shits about your car, your suit, or your fucking midlife crisis. Tell me what's going on with my money."

Shaw sat at the table, opened his briefcase, and pulled out some paperwork, which he placed on the table in front of La Monica and Lennox. Shaw pointed at the first page and said, "This is a comparison of the total number of accounts from when we started, what we had last year at this time, and where we are today. As you can see, we are very pleased with the growth of our accounts, which has given us the ability to increase our distributions and handle more of your incoming cash." Shaw pointed at the next page as he continued, "On this page you can see how your cash is moving between banks. If we want to significantly increase the amount of cash coming in, we will need to increase the frequency of these rotations to maximize how this is disbursed. To do that, we will need to grow the number of accounts at both of our other banks, like we did ours, or we would need to discuss the possibility of adding a fourth bank. Aiden, maybe you and I could talk through that idea if you have some thoughts on that." Shaw then pointed at the bottom line of the last page. "Lastly, this is your balance sheet as of April 30."

Lennox paid close attention to everything that Shaw showed him and said, "Allen, I think you are doing a good job with this. But I don't think this is the right time to add a fourth bank. I'm sure you've heard that Stratton got re-elected, and now he has Livingston working as his new attorney general. I've already heard he's sniffing around again and this time, he could do some real damage. We have been talking…" He indicated La Monica. "…and we are not going to send you any more cash." Lennox pointed at the balance sheet. "We want you to keep this money moving and hidden just as you've been doing. But be extra cautious and don't do anything differently that would draw any attention to us. Livingston is going to have the feds watching every suburban bank in the state. It's important that we stay focused on this for the next couple of years."

Later that August, Will and Carol were contacted again by their attorney and were told that a baby girl may become available for adoption in the next few weeks. They were overjoyed at the possibility of adding a daughter to their family, and in September that became a reality, when they brought a daughter, and sister, home from the hospital.

Will and Carol had prayed for children and decided that both children were special and chosen by God just for them, a belief and narrative they shared with both kids as they grew up.

To Will and Carol it seemed like forever ago when they sat together under that big oak tree and shared these dreams together. Now they had each other, a home of their own to establish roots, and a healthy and happy son and daughter. Carol cherished her time with her kids and loved them effortlessly, doting on their every need. With so many children in the neighborhood, days were filled with playdates and outings. And not a month went by without at least a couple of birthday parties to attend.

CHAPTER 17

The Distractions

1962

Time continued to tick by, and in most cases an ordinary day or week would be described as uneventful. However, Will and Carol were loving and dedicated parents who worked hard to make a great life for their children. They were busy with bills to pay, meals to prepare, and fulfilling every other necessary detail of daily life. To anyone looking in, none of it was particularly noteworthy, but it all fit neatly into what Will and Carol called "ordinary." So, the days turned to weeks and the weeks to months, but a constant throughout was their love for each other and their children. Will left the house each morning with a kiss for Carol and his kids, and he arrived home each night doing the same.

Carol returned home from her parents' house late on one of those "ordinary" Wednesday nights. As she drove by the bank, she noticed lights on. When she arrived home, she asked Will, "What's going on at the bank at this hour?"

Will asked, "What do you mean?"

Carol replied, "I just drove by there and I saw lights on. Would the cleaning crew be working this late?"

Will replied, "I don't think so. I'd better drive over and take a look."

Will walked to the front door and found it locked, so he started around the building to look in the windows. Unsure of what he might find inside, he walked quietly and peered in, hoping not to be seen. As he reached the window for Shaw's office, he looked in and saw Shaw seated at the conference table with two men with their backs to the window.

As Will watched from the corner of the window, he saw something different in Shaw that he had not seen before. It was a look on his face and a change in his mannerisms that concerned Will.

The following morning, Will went to Cain and closed the office door. Will said, "Gordon, late last night Carol saw lights on here, so I came by to see if everything was okay. I saw Allen here with two men in his office. Allen seemed different to me. Is everything okay?"

Cain asked nervously, "Did anyone see you?"

Will answered, "No, I just peeked in through the window."

"Did you see the men's faces?"

Will said, "No, they had their backs to me. But they were both well-dressed businessmen, so I did not suspect Allen was in any danger, but it seemed very weird to me."

Cain pressed, "So they didn't see you and you didn't see them?"

"No."

Cain said, "I know Allen has been working on some special projects. Let me talk to him, and I'll try to find out more about it. I'm sure everything is fine. I wouldn't worry about it. But for now, let's just keep this between us."

Later that morning Cain went to Shaw. "You had visitors last night."

Shaw asked, "How did you know?"

Cain answered, "Will just came into my office to tell me he came over here last night to check the lights that were on, and he saw you guys."

Shaw asked, "He saw them?"

"He didn't see their faces, but he saw you and thought it was odd that you were here so late. Just that he asked about it makes me nervous and makes me think he might start asking more questions. We're just lucky they didn't see him peeking in that window."

"Well, we're going to have to do something to distract Will," decided Shaw.

Cain asked, "What do you mean?"

"Let me tell you a story about when my father took me to see the magician, Harry Blackstone at the Goodman Theatre. Blackstone filled the place, and as he started doing card tricks and his famous dancing handkerchief, some guy sitting in the first row would yell out 'He's palming it' or 'It's on a wire,' trying to let everyone in the audience know that he knew how Blackstone was doing his tricks. Then Blackstone stopped everything and invited the man up onto the stage and worked him into the act for the rest of the show. And it was great. One of the best shows I've ever seen. On our way home I asked, 'Why did he invite that man that was being so rude up to the stage to be part of the show?' My father answered, 'He didn't have any choice. He needed to distract that man with something different. If he had let him sit there trying to figure out every trick or let him yell out how he was doing it, he would have ruined the show for everyone else. By inviting him up on stage he was able to distract him and put himself back in control of the show. Blackstone is a professional performer and knew he had to change that man's perspective. That wasn't the first time someone yelled out during one of his shows, and he was prepared for it.'"

Cain responded, "I don't understand."

Shaw said, "I think it's time we invite Will up on stage."

A FEW WEEKS LATER, WILL AND CAROL'S ROUTINE WAS interrupted when the phone rang. Will was lying on the couch watching TV with his son asleep on his chest. With the baby already in bed, Carol jumped up quickly from her chair to get the phone before the ringing woke the kids. Will only heard, "Oh, hi, Allen. He's right here. Hang on, I'll get him."

Will handed off a still-sleeping toddler to Carol and said, "Hi, Allen."

Shaw said, "Will, I'm sorry to call so late, but I'm setting up a very important meeting for tomorrow morning at 8 a.m., and I need you to be there."

Will answered, "Okay, I'll be there. See you in the morning at 8."

As he hung up, Carol asked, "What's that all about?"

Will said, "I don't know, but I need to go in early."

The following morning, Will found the bank door unlocked and the lobby empty and quiet. The lights were off, but he could hear voices coming from the back conference room, so he made his way in. As he entered, he was greeted by Shaw. "Good morning, Will."

There were three other men present whom Will did not immediately recognize. Shaw introduced them from his left to right. "Will, this is Arthur Denholm, Jerome Margate, and Richard Stillman."

Will shook each of their hands and said, "Good morning. Nice to meet you, gentlemen."

Shaw invited, "Will, please join us." Will sat at the table as Shaw continued, "All of these men sit on the board of directors for our bank." Shaw paused briefly and offered a quick smile before he continued, "We don't do this frequently, so I wanted to invite members of the board to participate in this milestone. The growth of our bank since you joined us is well documented, and we all believe that it is directly due to your persistence, hard work, and dedication. Will, over the past few weeks I have been meeting with members of the board, and we are in unanimous agreement that you be promoted to the position of vice president." Shaw presented Will with a new door plate that read, "Will Hays—Vice President."

"You will be moving upstairs, so you can put that on the door of your new office, and you'll also need these." Shaw slid a box of new business cards across the table to him. "You will now be managing all new business for this bank, and you will be working directly with the board on ideas for branch expansion."

Will cracked open the box, peeked inside, and saw "Will Hays—Vice President" printed on the cards.

Shaw continued, "Lastly…" He slid a sheet of paper toward him. "…this promotion comes with a pay raise. This is a summary of your new salary and compensation structure, which will take effect immediately." The four men stood in unison and clapped their hands in applause.

Will was overwhelmed. His eyes started to well up as he shook each of their hands and offered each man a personal and heartfelt "Thank you." Will stopped at Shaw and with tears in his eyes said, "I don't know what to say. How do I ever thank you for this?"

Shaw told him, "Will, today it's us that are thanking you. You have earned every bit of this. Now go home, share this news with Carol and the kids, and take the day. We'll talk more tomorrow."

Will arrived back at the house just about an hour after he left, and Carol had both kids in the kitchen fixing them breakfast. She unexpectedly heard the front door open and called out, "Is that you?" She waited for a reply, but none came. So, she peeked around the corner and saw Will standing at the front door with tears in his eyes. She exclaimed, "Oh, my God, what happened?" Will couldn't answer and just continued to stand there silently. Carol was getting worried and left the kids in their highchairs to walk over to Will. She cried out again, "What is it?"

Will looked down at the business card in his hand. Carol grabbed the card and read what was printed on it. "Oh, my God!" she shouted and wrapped her arms around Will.

Her outburst startled the kids who both started to cry, so her celebration was short-lived as they hustled back to the kitchen to comfort them.

With two small children now who Carol needed to transport, the family's need for a second car had increased. This promotion would help make that happen. The following morning, Will walked into Cain's office as Cain said, "Hey, congratulations, Will. Allen told me the good news this morning."

Will said, "Gordon, none of this would have been possible without you. I don't know how I can ever thank you."

"You don't owe me anything. I got you in the door here, but everything else is all you. You got this promotion because you earned it, and you deserve it."

Will listened and was grateful for the kind words as he began to let a small grin out and asked, "You know anybody that sells Cadillacs?"

Cain shouted, "Now you're talkin'!"

Will had always associated Cadillacs with success and always dreamed of owning a new Cadillac one day. In addition to sheer desire, he felt it was important to project the image of success that this new promotion required. He again completed a finance application through the bank and again was quickly approved. He decided on a 1962 Cadillac Fleetwood. The polished black paint looked as if you could swim in it, and all the chrome trim added to the look of luxury and success. The car was so long, the salesman joked that the front and rear bumpers were in different zip codes. Will slid into the black leather interior and drove home looking over the long hood of his brand-new Cadillac.

This promotion provided some credibility to Will's accomplishments, and not long after the promotion announcement, the Chamber of Commerce members nominated Will for president of the chamber. And in a unanimous vote, he was elected president of the Chamber of Commerce in November.

That following summer, Will was invited to be the grand marshal of the annual Grayslake Fourth of July parade. But rather than ride in a car, as the grand marshals had in the past, most of whom had been much older than Will, Will and Carol decided to walk the parade route, both proudly holding one of their small children in their arms. This was the exact image that GNB had wanted from Will from the beginning. A handsome young family and a gleaming example of the American dream.

Cain stood alone outside the front door of the bank and watched the celebration as the parade approached. He smiled and waved at Will, Carol, and the kids as they walked by when Shaw pushed the door open to join Cain and stood next to him. Cain looked at Shaw and said, "Hello, you just missed Will and Carol."

Shaw replied, "Lennox just called. La Monica is thinking of retiring."

Cain immediately looked worried, and while shaking his head in disgust, said, "Well, that's not good for us." And with the marching band now playing loudly directly in front of the bank, Cain turned away and went inside without saying another word.

After his promotion, Will began to expand his reach into neighboring towns as he worked to get the message of GNB in front of as many people outside of Grayslake as possible. He brought Cain in on larger investment presentations, and they also tackled some larger corporate proposals. Will had engaged with so many people in neighboring communities that branch expansion became a viable possibility.

Many of the people he spoke to were so intrigued with how Will described Grayslake that they decided to move into town. So, Will and Carol started a new social club that they affectionately called "The Welcome Wagon." On the second Saturday of each month, they hosted new residents in social mixers at their home. Will and Carol made introductions to others in the community and helped newcomers acclimate to their new surroundings in Grayslake.

IT WAS JUST AFTER 3 P.M. ON A LATE AUGUST FRIDAY afternoon when Shaw called Will into his office.

Will walked in and jokingly asked, "What are you still doing here on a Friday?"

Shaw answered while smiling, "I could ask you the same thing."

"Well, I figured you would be out on the golf course today," replied Will.

"I didn't play today. They said it was going to rain, so I moved our tee time to tomorrow morning."

They both laughed as they looked out the window at what had become a beautiful sunny afternoon.

Shaw continued, "We're playing River's Edge tomorrow morning at 8 a.m., and now I need a fourth for our foursome."

Will knew the club well and that it was a very prestigious "members only" country club. "I would love to join you, but I don't think they will let me play with you guys since I'm not a member, and I don't want to cause any problems for you there."

Shaw stood and said emphatically, "You're playing!" as he walked over to Will and handed him a River's Edge membership keycard with "Will Hays" engraved on the front. "Meet me there at 7:15 so we'll have time to get your clubs cleaned and get you set up with a good caddy."

Will didn't know what to say. This was not a perk from the bank; Shaw had done this on his own. He had sponsored him for this membership and paid his initiation fee out of his pocket. Memberships like these cost thousands of dollars, and the club only allowed the very best of the best in its doors.

Shaw asked, "So, will I see you in the morning?"

Will appeared shocked but replied, "Definitely. Thank you, Allen. I'll see you then." Will just stood there wondering again how a poor farm boy from rural Illinois had this great life that now included membership in such a prestigious country club.

As new members, Will and Carol met Shaw and his wife, Delores, at the club for lunch or dinner at least once or twice a week. They grew to be quite popular, and Carol made an entirely new group of friends. She was constantly being invited out to coffee, brunch, or lunch, and even started attending Tupperware, Avon, and jewelry parties with Delores and her newfound friends.

Carol enjoyed the jewelry parties the most because they involved high-quality costume jewelry just like she used to wear when she played dress-up with her old friend Margie in high school plays back in LaSalle. Carol attended so frequently that one of the hostesses from Judy Lee Jewels approached her and asked if she was interested in hosting parties of her own to earn some extra money and get bigger discounts on items she purchased in the future. The hostess told her that it was a good company and that she thought Carol would be a perfect host. Carol was intrigued and could not wait to talk it over with Will when she got home that night. They sat at the kitchen table, and Carol laid out the brochures that discussed the products, pricing structures, costs, and compensation plans. It was a business model based on volume, which meant the more you sold, the more you would earn. This was not a get-rich-quick proposition, and they both realized that a lot of time and effort would be required for this to be successful.

But neither was afraid of hard work or a challenge, so they both dove in and gave this a try. They submitted their application, and a couple of weeks later the promotional packet and jewelry sample case arrived.

Carol started right away by networking with Delores and her new friends from the club, and in her first two weeks, Carol had scheduled at least two parties every weekend for the next six months. Will helped her get set up with portable tables and lights for the jewelry displays. Will had one big concern with their plan, and that was that Carol would be doing a lot of driving at night and would almost always be alone. He came up with a solution and provided her with her own "bodyguard." It was an inflatable "man" that they affectionately named Chester (because the balloon was shaped in just the upper torso of a man). Chester had a heavy sand base to keep him in the seat, and "he" would wear one of Will's fedoras so that to any passing vehicle, it looked like an actual man was in the passenger seat next to Carol.

Will and Carol formed their own company and were incorporated. They both worked hard at this, and by the end of 1963 were already challenging sales records. To help grow the business quickly, any earnings were reinvested back into the business to purchase more and more product.

CHAPTER 18

The Panic

1964

A new year was now well underway, and Carol continued to shatter monthly sales records. Corporate executives were so impressed with her effort that they personally visited them in Grayslake to encourage them to keep going and told them that the yearly sales leaders would be crowned "King and Queen" of Judy Lee Jewels. Will and Carol pushed hard for that win, and though it meant more time away from her kids, Carol increased her show schedule to sometimes five or six a week. Will and Carol won that title, and the prize package included a brand-new 1964 Ford Mustang Coupe. Carol chose hers in Caspian blue, her favorite color, and then jokingly told Will that he could pick the color of next year's Mustang.

With the new business a success and the kids getting older, Will and Carol started to talk more frequently about needing a larger house with more room for the kids to play, for entertaining friends, and to host larger jewelry parties. And now with a third car, they really needed added garage space as well.

Will told Cain about Carol's recent success and awards and shared their idea of moving into a larger house. He asked for some advice on how he could make that happen.

Cain said, "Let's sit down in the next couple of weeks, and we can talk through that idea."

LIVINGSTON WAS AT HIS OFFICE DESK EARLY ON A Monday morning, talking on the phone with his father who had called to tell him about a company in Bridgeport closing after nearly sixty years in business. Livingston responded to that news by asking, "What's he going to do? Didn't he just build that huge house in Bucktown?"

His father answered, "Sam, just because a business loses money or even goes out of business doesn't mean the owner is broke. A lot of wealthy people need to sometimes lose money as a way to keep money."

That statement triggered something in Livingston's mind as he said, "Thanks, Dad. I have to go. I'll call you tomorrow." He hurried his father off the phone and hung up. Livingston called his secretary on the intercom and said, "Helen, get the team together. I want everyone in the conference room in an hour."

His team of investigators and prosecutors were all waiting for him as he walked in with purpose. He began speaking before he reached his seat. "I think maybe we have been looking at this from the entirely wrong angle. We have been spending so much time looking for banks that were either making more money or moving more than they should. Let's look at this from a different perspective. Let's start looking at banks that are losing more money than they should be. Maybe some of those banks are showing larger losses on their balance sheets to help offset or hide cash they have coming in off the books.

"Do any of you remember that bank in Grayslake that doubled its number of accountholders in just two or three years? I think we looked hard at them a while ago, but nothing ever panned out. I still think something might be off there, so let's look at them again, but this time let's look closer at what they are reporting as losses.

"And let's also look at every bank within a fifty-mile radius of them to see if anyone near them is also reporting any big losses. These banks might be part of a network, so let's be thorough on this. And I don't want to just see who is showing losses, I want to see how many accountholders they have, and I want to see median incomes for those accountholders. And if we do find something, let's get the Federal Reserve to get a report on all their cash movements for the past twenty-four months. Let's get moving on this. We don't have much time left."

Just weeks later, Livingston was at his desk as his intercom buzzed, and his secretary said, "Sir, Investigator Donlon is here to see you."

Livingston replied, "Send him in."

Donlon burst into the office and blurted out confidently, "It's Round Lake National Bank."

Livingston stood up and asked, "What did you find?"

Donlon emphatically said, "Over two million in reported losses last year with only 375 account holders, and all those with just a median income of $3,900. There is no way those folks up there can afford to lose that much money on investments."

Livingston replied, "Nice work, Jerry. Find out as much as you can about the ownership group there, and let's do backgrounds on the board of directors, the bank president, and each of the branch employees. Someone up there is going to talk."

The phone rang in La Monica's office as he walked inside from a cool but sun-soaked terrace. He picked it up and answered, "Hello."

Lennox was on the line. "Sal, we have a problem in Grayslake. I just got off the phone with Shaw, and he's in a panic. He tells me that Barnes, the president of our bank in Round Lake, has not been in the office since early Monday morning and is not returning any of his phone calls. Shaw says he spoke with a couple of the tellers up there who told him that Barnes met with a man when the bank first opened Monday morning. Based on the descriptions they provided, it sounds like it could have been Livingston. The tellers mentioned that the man was wearing a plaid vest with his suit."

La Monica shouted, "Goddammit! Get Shaw in here right fucking now. I want both of you in Lake Forest in an hour!"

Lennox called Shaw and asked, "Is Cain in his office today?"

Shaw answered, "Yes, why?"

"Is anything, and I mean anything, out of the ordinary up there?" Lennox pressed.

Shaw became increasingly nervous and said, "Other than Barnes not calling me back, no, nothing. Everything else is fine here."

"Okay, be in Lake Forest in one hour. Don't be late."

Shaw's nerves were getting the better of him, and he asked Lennox frantically, "Is La Monica going to kill me? Aiden, I need you to tell me, what am I walking into?"

Lennox was never one to panic, so he told Shaw in a calm and firm voice, "Allen, if you don't calm down and get your shit together before this meeting, I'll kill you myself. Don't get ahead of yourself and fuck this up for all of us. I'll see you there in an hour."

Shaw walked into La Monica's office and sat at the table across from Lennox who was also joined by Mike Baker, who had been promoted to the head of La Monica's entire security detail.

La Monica started by abruptly looking at Shaw and saying, "You have close to 19 million dollars of my money in your banks, and I want you to tell me right now if I have something to worry about. Is this guy Barnes a problem or not?"

Shaw looked as if he couldn't decide whether he wanted to cry or throw up as he said, "It's unusual for him to not be in the bank or return my phone calls. I… I think he might be a problem. He knows what we are doing and exactly how we are doing it. Cain and I ran the numbers before I left, and there are just over 6 million dollars in the Round Lake bank right now. Cain is already working to move as much of that back to us as quietly and quickly as he can. And just to be safe, we are also pulling everything back from Hainesville as well. By the end of the day, we will have all your money back in Grayslake."

Lennox looked at Shaw. "At this point, we need to assume that Barnes is talking to Livingston. Hell, Livingston might even have him in federal protection by now. Allen, you and Cain focus on getting all our money back to Grayslake, and I want a call from you as soon as that happens. Then get all our money out of the accounts and make sure it's secured and can't be found. Allen, make no mistake, if we lose even one fucking dollar of our money because Barnes talked to Livingston, the feds, or whoever, I'll kill

Barnes, you, and the guy from Hainseville. And I won't lose a minute of fucking sleep over it."

The tension in the room was interrupted when the phone rang. La Monica walked to his desk and picked it up. "Hello. Hold on. Shaw, it's for you. I'm not your fucking secretary, so this better be fucking important."

Shaw walked over and took the phone. "Hello?" He stood listening for a moment with his head down. Then suddenly, he lifted his head in surprise and asked, "Are you sure? You're positive? Okay, I'll let them know. Thanks, Gordon."

Shaw turned back to the table and said, "That was Cain. Round Lake is sending back their money, but 1 million of it is missing." He took a deep breath and continued, "I'm just thinking out loud, but could it be possible that Livingston went to see Barnes Monday morning and that visit rattled him enough that rather than rat us all out, he took a million dollars and ran off somewhere?"

Lennox looked directly at Baker. "Mike, hurry up and get going. Barnes has a million dollars and a two-day head start." He added, "Mike, if possible, bring Barnes and the money back here to me. If not, just bring the fucking money."

Baker nodded and replied, "You got it, boss."

Lennox turned back to Shaw and said, "Listen, we can't assume that Barnes hasn't talked to Livingston, so we need to proceed with the plan to safeguard the cash. Just pull it all back, and we'll just sit on it for a while until we sort all this out."

IT WAS JUST AFTER 11 A.M. ON A BEAUTIFUL, SUNNY, AND warm mid-August morning in Miami. Mike Baker and a colleague were sitting in a parked 1964 Chevrolet Impala, watching a beachside bungalow from across the street, which was lined on both sides with palm trees. Baker had clearly been awake all night, and although he still wore his sport coat, his tie was loosened and the top button of his dress shirt undone. With the high humidity and the morning temperature rising, his forehead and face had begun to perspire as well. Baker sipped from his coffee cup; he had his left hand out the driver's window holding a lit cigarette when he saw the front screen door of the bungalow across the street open.

He took one last drag from his cigarette before he extinguished it in the now nearly overflowing ashtray below the front dashboard. Baker's partner was asleep in the passenger seat with his hat tilted down covering his eyes as Baker smacked his shoulder and said, "Felix, wake up. That's him."

Barnes, a middle-aged man trying way too hard to fit in by wearing a teal-green Hawaiian shirt printed with bright pink flamingos, white-and-gray checkered Bermuda shorts, and black dress socks with his sandals, could not have looked more like an out-of-towner. Though stocky and a bit plump around the middle, he was comfortable enough that his head, forearms, and legs were bright red from a sunburn. He walked down the front stairs of the bungalow holding a folded beach chair and turned right, heading east toward the beach. As Barnes turned the corner at the end of the block, Baker and Felix got out of the car. Felix stretched his neck and back before he straightened his necktie and adjusted his hat. Baker told him, "Don't forget the bible." Felix opened the back door and leaned in to retrieve it as Baker said, "I'll find a way in through the back."

Felix walked confidently up to the front door and knocked firmly. He had a medium build but was still slender and wore a black suit, white dress shirt, black tie, and black hat. Felix stood at the front door with the bible cradled against his chest in his left hand and waited for someone to answer. When no one did, he just waited on the front porch quietly.

Felix was startled when a neighbor called out to him from next door, "Hey there, mister, can I help you with something?"

Felix turned with a big smile and broadcasted loudly, "Hello there, friend, I am spreading the good word of our Lord and Savior, Jesus Christ. Do you have some time to sit down and discuss your salvation with me?

"I would be happy to come over right now if you have some time to talk, and afterward, I will leave you with your own complimentary bible [he held the bible in his right hand for the neighbor to see] so you can start reading the good word of our Lord and praying right away!"

The neighbor, wearing a robe over his pajamas and slippers, had already picked up his newspaper from his walkway, which he waved for Felix to see and said, "No time right now. Got to get back inside to read the paper and have a late breakfast." The neighbor seemed like he couldn't get back inside fast enough and looked as if he regretted even calling out to the stranger in the first place.

Felix yelled back, "Okay, then. God bless you, sir, and remember, Jesus loves you. Have a blessed day."

As Felix watched the neighbor reenter his house, Baker appeared in the bushes at the corner of the house and whispered, "Get the car and meet me around back." Felix drove around to the back alley and saw Baker standing about halfway down it, holding a small suitcase. Felix picked him up, and as Felix sped away, Baker rolled down his window and threw the bible out as he said, "Stop up here somewhere so I can count this cash."

Felix pulled over at the corner, and Baker got into the back seat to start the count. Felix sat quietly, drumming his fingers nervously on the steering wheel while listening to the radio. Baker mumbled numbers under his breath as he looked up, seemingly agitated by Felix's distracting drumming. Baker had stacks of cash piled up on the seat around him as he said, "Looks like it's just short about $19,000. Let's go find that asshole, Barnes."

The turquoise Impala drove slowly along the beachfront road as Baker looked out his window, intently searching the crowd for Barnes' brightly colored Hawaiian shirt.

He finally recognized his target and said calmly, "There he is." Felix parked as they both adjusted their mirrors to watch Barnes behind them.

Baker and Felix watched Barnes all day as he sat alone under a bright blue beach umbrella sipping cold drinks from the nearby hotel bar. They watched as a beautiful young woman with blonde hair and tan skin in a very small white bikini stopped to talk to Barnes. The young woman returned a few minutes later carrying a cold cocktail on her small serving tray. This repeated every forty-five to fifty minutes for the remainder of the afternoon and evening. Baker grew impatient and made his way over to the hotel bar, where he approached the young woman, then pointed toward Barnes and asked, "Is the guy sitting over there under the blue umbrella a guest in your hotel?"

She answered, "Artie? No, he's a local but he tips me with a $100 bill every time I bring him a drink or a sandwich, so we let him sit there."

Baker asked, "How long has he been sitting there?"

"He's been here every day for the last couple of weeks.

I was supposed to be off today, but I can't afford to not be here. You know what I mean?"

Baker answered, "Thanks, doll. Do me a favor and don't tell Artie I asked about him." He handed her a $100 bill and walked back to the car.

Baker got in and said, "This fucking guy is spending $1,000 a day just sitting on the beach, getting drunk, and looking at girls."

Felix, growing impatient, told Baker, "We have the cash. Let's just ice this fucker and go home."

Baker replied, "Just hang on. It's his last day. Let him enjoy it." As the sun began to set, people started leaving the beach, and Baker and Felix watched as Barnes, now intoxicated, awkwardly stumbled through the sand as he made his way back up to the road from the beach.

As Barnes started his walk back to his house, Baker and Felix knew where he was headed, and the turquoise Impala drove slowly past Barnes to get ahead of him. As Barnes turned the corner onto his street, he saw the silhouette of Felix standing on the sidewalk under a streetlight. Barnes dropped his beach chair, his shoulders slumped, and he whispered to himself, "Oh, no." As Barnes stood motionless and seemingly resigned to his fate, it allowed Baker the time to move in silently behind him. In the darkness, Baker's face was barely illuminated by the streetlight half a block away as he quickly reached around Barnes' neck and held his head tight as the shiny point of an ice pick pierced the skin and muscle of Barnes' neck. Baker shoved it deeper into Barnes' neck and pierced the brain stem and spinal cord. It killed Barnes instantly and, most importantly to Baker, quietly as he guided Barnes' lifeless body down to the ground and pulled him into the bushes and out of sight.

It was just after 9:00 a.m., and the bank had just opened as Shaw entered through the front door and made his usual walk through the lobby toward his office. Cain saw Shaw enter and followed him, closed the door, and shuffled around nervously in front of Shaw's desk with his hands in his pockets.

Shaw asked, "What is it?"

Cain looked out the window to avoid eye contact with Shaw as he said, "Barnes is dead. They found his wallet and shoes near his beach chair in Miami, Florida. They think he drowned. You and I both know he didn't. At least not by accident."

Shaw leaned back in his chair, put his hands on his head, looked up at the ceiling, and quietly said, "Fuck."

Cain looked directly at Shaw and asked, "Allen, how is this all going to end?"

Shaw asked, "What do you mean?"

"All of this. Lennox, the Outfit, the money... All of it. Is that how it is going to end for us too? Shot in the head, our throat cut, or drowned in our own bathtub?"

"Why would it end?"

Cain said, "We've been doing this for six years now, and we never talked about doing this forever. You told me that La Monica was thinking about stepping down soon, and Lennox is getting older. I'm worried about who might take over for him when he's done. I'm afraid that we're just in way too deep with this. The way I see it, one of two things is going to happen here. Either the Outfit pulls all their cash out, or we get raided by the feds. If the mob does pull their cash, it won't take them long to figure out that money is missing, and they'll have us killed. And if the feds raid us, they'll confiscate everything, and we'll end up in prison for the rest of our lives. Both are bad outcomes for us. There is no way for us to get out or start over. And even if we could get out, we're way too old to start over."

Shaw replied, "Well, it seems to me that you've been giving this quite a bit of thought. So, what do you have in mind?"

"I do have an idea, but I'm worried about Will."

Shaw asked, "Will? What do you mean? What does Will have to do with any of this?"

Cain answered, "He's young. He has a family. Not to mention he's been here with us the whole time. Everyone, and I mean everyone, is going to think he was in on this. We can't just hang him out to dry. He's a good man, and he's been a great friend to both of us. We need to look out for him."

Shaw asked, "So, what's your idea?"

"I think we should run soon," replied Cain. "Let's take as much cash as we can and just disappear. Right now, I think I can access close to $15 million. You and Delores take half. I'll take the other half, and we go."

"Barnes just ran with $1 million, and they found him in a matter of weeks and killed him. How are we supposed to run with $7.5 million in cash? Are we just going to put it in big suitcases and lug it through airports? And where are we going to go?"

Cain said, "Barnes panicked and was stupid. He made a spur-of-the-moment decision and went to his mother-in-law's house in Florida. I'm surprised they didn't find him sooner. We are smarter than that, and we have some time to give this some thought and make a good plan. And it doesn't matter where we go. At our age we only need to stay hidden for what, maybe twenty years or so? With this much money we can easily do that in Mexico, Europe, wherever." Cain continued pacing as he thought. "As for the cash, you are right about that. We can't take that much…" Cain paused. "But diamonds, gemstones…jewelry. That would work. What if we took all the jewelry that Delores has been buying from Carol over the last couple of years to an actual jeweler and started having the costume stones replaced with real gemstones and real diamonds? It will be much easier to travel with jewelry, and then we can just sell stones for cash as we need it over time." Cain nodded to himself as if to say he liked his idea. "And if we need more jewelry, Delores can always buy more from Carol over the next few weeks."

Shaw leaned back in his chair and put both hands behind his neck. "Interesting…. Maybe that could actually work."

Shaw continued, "So, we would need to start stockpiling cash now so we can have it converted to diamonds and gems over the next few weeks. I'll have to start working on finding a jeweler that can make these changes for us." He leaned forward, put his elbows on the desk, and asked, "Now what about Will?"

Cain replied, "Well, I've been thinking about how we can keep Will out of this. The only way I see to get him out free and clear is to make him a victim in all of this."

"What do you mean, a victim?"

Cain said, "Like an actual victim. I will need to leave plenty of evidence that shows that the cash we are taking will be from legitimate clients' investments and not just mob money. A couple of weeks ago, Will asked me for some advice on purchasing a bigger house, so I am going to get him to make a huge investment with me using his current house as collateral." Cain looked at Shaw and said, "I'll need you to help me fudge the numbers on the appraisal so we can over-inflate his home's value and exaggerate his level of equity. Then I will get him to invest as much of it as possible. He will be way over-leveraged on the investment, and when we are gone, he will be bankrupt. He will have nothing left."

"Are you crazy?" asked Shaw. "You can't do that to him!"

"Allen, think about it. It's perfect. He will be left with nothing. No job, no house, no cars, no money, and the people in town will vilify him because he was the one who brought them to us. But if he has no money and nothing left, then the feds and the Outfit will have no other choice than to see he was not in on it." Cain continued, "Will is one of the most decent men I have ever met. He has the strongest convictions of anyone I know. He has a deep love of family and a remarkable faith in God. I know that this will devastate him, but I also know Will, and he will survive this. And I promise, I will find a way to make this right with him later."

Later that same afternoon, Will stopped in at Cain's office, and they sat together to go through his finances.

Cain asked, "What kind of house are you thinking about?"

Will reminded Cain of the story of the first time he walked Carol home from high school and that he never imagined being able to live in a house like the one that Carol grew up in. Will told him what Carol said to him that day, "Maybe someday you'll buy me a house like this." He told Cain, "That someday is today. I want to find the perfect house and surprise her with it. So tell me what I have to do to make that happen, and please remember that this is a surprise, so let's just keep this between us. I don't want Carol to know anything about what I'm doing for her."

When Cain heard that, the look on his face suggested that he might be second-guessing his plan to victimize Will, but then he quickly reset to the idea of self-preservation and told Will that he liked the idea of finding a larger house and that he thought with the right down payment, they could afford the bigger house right away. Cain added, "From a cash flow point of view, it is unlikely that you will be able to access equity in any new house for at least a few years. It typically takes five to seven years to develop any type of usable equity on property when you have a maximum mortgage and a minimum down payment."

Cain told Will that this would be a perfect time for him to invest the equity that he had already accumulated in his current house and that a larger investment like that could provide him with a bigger return in just a few months. He also said that the money gained could not only provide him with the down payment he needed to get the new house, but he could also have enough to pay off some other bills, including the Cadillac. Cain told Will that a large down payment would immediately show as equity in the new house and that equity could be useful if he needed to access cash to help grow the jewelry business in the future.

Cain also told him that he could have as much as $30,000 in equity in his house right now and that if he invested the maximum amount, he could be in for a big payday. Over the next day or two, Will gave this idea some serious thought and daydreamed of walking into this big, beautiful house with Carol and the kids. He had faith in Cain, so he decided to go big and completed the second mortgage application for the maximum amount of $30,000.

Cain called him later that week to let him know the application was approved, and the second mortgage closed later that month. Will was issued a bank check for $30,000, which he signed over, along with a personal check for $5,000 that nearly cleaned out his savings account. Will kept working, integrating this most recent personal investment story with prospective clients as he encouraged them to invest their money with Cain. Will would check in with Cain periodically on how his investment was doing, and each time Cain would provide his usual smile, a big thumbs-up, and say, "Going great. You might want to look at a bigger house."

CHAPTER 19

The Devastation

1965

It was an overcast and rainy March morning. Cain had called Will the previous evening to let him know that the weekly Tuesday staff meeting, scheduled for that morning, would be canceled and that they would make it up the following week. Will woke up at his usual time, but today, with no need to be in early for the meeting, he sat down to a leisurely breakfast with his family and played with the kids for an hour or so before he kissed Carol and both kids goodbye and headed off to work. He arrived at the bank a few minutes later and noticed six plain black sedans and two Grayslake police cars parked by the front door. As he got to the front doors, he found them locked, and a handwritten note was taped to the glass that read, "Bank Closed Today."

Will was digging in his pocket for his keys when the door was unlocked and pushed open from inside by a man in a black suit. The man showed him a badge and identified himself as Special Agent Meyer from the Chicago office of the FBI. The agent asked him for his identification, and Will identified himself with his driver's license and bank ID card. After he entered, the agent re-locked the door behind him.

Will saw that the lobby lights were off and that other bank employees were gathered near a desk in the corner being watched by uniformed police officers. He heard someone from within that group say, "That's one of them." Agent Meyer heard the same thing and quickly grabbed Will by the arm and escorted him to a secluded office in the back of the bank. As they walked by the conference room, Will saw another three or four agents seated around the table with stacks of file folders and loose documents scattered about.

Will became increasingly confused and continued to ask Meyer what was going on. Meyer took an extremely aggressive posture in his questioning of Will and made it known that they suspected he had some level of involvement in Cain's scheme. Meyer questioned him for more than an hour as Will repeatedly told agents that he had no idea what was going on. The other agent in the room looked at Meyer and shrugged as if asking "What next?"

Finally, Meyer told Will why they were there. "The FBI and the Illinois attorney general have been working with the Federal Reserve Bank and the Department of Justice for several months investigating unusual financial activity at your bank. We finally secured a subpoena yesterday that documents were to be turned over this morning. Our investigation is focused on a man named Gordon Cain."

When Will heard that, all the air left his lungs, and he felt like he had been kicked in the chest. Shocked at this news, he sat dumbfounded.

Meyer told Will, "We had an appointment to interview Allen Shaw this morning. But when we arrived, he was not here, so we went to his house and performed a cursory check of the premises. It appeared to us that no one was home, so we have agents standing by at his house waiting for a judge to sign a search warrant so we can perform a thorough search of the inside and the surrounding property. We went to Cain's residence as well, but it appeared that he was not at home either. We have agents standing by at that location as well. The agents working in the conference room are reviewing existing documents on a preliminary forensic audit of your bank's records. The initial indication is that millions of dollars are missing from your bank." Lastly, Meyer asked, "Have you ever heard the name Aiden Lennox?"

Will answered, "No, who is it?"

Meyer replied, "Nobody. It's not important."

Will could not believe this was happening, and he was humbled, humiliated, and hurt to think that agents thought that he would have any part in this criminal activity. He cooperated fully and told agents everything that he had seen and discussed with Cain over the past six years. Throughout the questioning, Will thought about all the money that he too had given Cain as an investment, and he grew more convinced that his money was now gone forever. All these events had put his job, home, family, and entire life in jeopardy.

Will told Meyer about the $35,000 of his own money he gave Cain just three months earlier and that he would give them whatever information he could to help in the investigation.

Will was emotionally and mentally devastated by this and was clearly broken. He drove home trying to think of how he was going to tell Carol everything that had just happened. The list of devastations was gigantic and growing with every minute. Will arrived home and asked Carol to sit with him at the kitchen table. They sat and stared quietly at each other, neither one knowing exactly what to say or even how to begin. Will looked at Carol through tears as he tried to start from the beginning but could only get a few words at a time out before breaking down again. But somehow, he managed to get it all out.

Will told Carol that he had taken out a second mortgage on the house and had emptied their savings account. The fact that he thought this investment would help set them up in a big, beautiful house like the one Carol grew up in seemed, and was, irrelevant. They were ruined financially, and his job at GNB was certainly over.

Carol had tears running down her face as she asked, "What are we going to do? We don't have any money, and now we are going to lose the house. Where are we going to go? We've got two small kids. What are we going to do?"

And in that split-second, Will found himself transported back in time when he was hiding under that dining room table as a small six-year-old boy. But this time instead of watching his mother crying, it was Carol's face that he saw sitting at that old farmhouse kitchen table.

Startled at the sight of this, young Will flinched and bumped one of the chairs, causing it to bang into the table. Suddenly he saw the back of his father's deerskin barn coat start to slowly turn toward him, and then his father leaned down further and further until he looked directly at him. Young Will gasped in surprise as it was not his father's face he saw looking at him, it was his own.

Will realized that he was not the six-year-old hiding under the table this time. He had become his father, and now it was him that caused all this pain. It was his beloved Carol with that same look of "pain and disappointment" on her face.

A devastated Will realized that all this was his doing and that he had allowed everything they had worked so hard for to be taken from them. He punished himself by thinking that he was greedy and unsatisfied with all that God had provided for them.

Agents were at the bank every day for the next three weeks as they reviewed every document, deposit, and withdrawal since Cain and Shaw joined the bank. The agents were leaving the bank every night with boxes of evidence, and their early conclusions were that Will had no knowledge of what Cain and Shaw had done and that he had no part in this criminal enterprise. In the end, the FBI forensic audit of all bank records showed that Cain and Shaw disappeared with nearly $15.2 million.

The FBI concluded that because large quantities of mob cash were undocumented, the total number could have exceeded $20 million.

After an exhaustive investigation by the FBI, Illinois State Police, the Federal Reserve Bank, and the DOJ, federal, state, and county prosecutors concluded that there was absolutely no evidence that Will was involved in the crimes perpetrated by Allen Shaw and Gordon Cain.

However, the community of Grayslake did not share those findings. Hundreds of people from the community who brought their money to invest with GNB did so because they trusted Will. For all those who invested with Cain, their money was gone forever. These were people just like Will. Hard-working and honest people who wanted better for their families and had trusted Will to that end. That was the hardest pill for him to swallow. His community trusted him, and he felt that he had let them down.

The aftermath showed that Will had a first and second mortgage on their home that totaled $42,000. Agents discovered that Shaw had changed the appraised value on the second mortgage documents to increase and maximize the investment amount. Their home had an actual appraised value of just under $19,000. So, the house would go into foreclosure, and they still had about $4,000 left to pay on the Cadillac. So now they could not afford to keep that either.

People around town who invested with GNB, and even those who didn't, took out their frustrations on Will, Carol, and even the kids. There was finger-pointing, scowls, and exclusion at every turn. Throughout all the good times, they had plenty of friends, but now in tough times, there was no one. Even at church and around the club, they could not escape the nasty looks and jeers, and it became increasingly evident that there was no way they could stay in Grayslake.

By the beginning of May, it was over, and everything was gone. Will had resigned from his job. The house and the Cadillac were surrendered to the bank to avoid foreclosure and repossession. Every jewelry party that Carol had scheduled was canceled. All the jewelry inventory was returned, along with the Mustang, to help offset costs, restocking fees, taxes, and all other charges related to closing the business. Even the Chevy Bel Air was sold off to a local mechanic so they would have a little cash on hand.

With nowhere to go, Carol found a small two-bedroom apartment that was available immediately about ten miles away in the neighboring town of Libertyville. They were both too proud to retreat to their parents, and their families offered very little support or empathy toward what they were going through. There was even a sense of "I told you so" and "I knew this was too good to be true" looming beneath the surface within both families.

The kids' rooms at the house were emptied and the wallpaper and curtains that they so meticulously used to decorate the rooms left behind. Every mark on the door jamb that signified the kids' growth would soon be painted over by the new owner, and Carol looked out her kitchen window for the last time with tears streaming down her face as both kids cried while being carried out to the car. Every memory of their life in that house was now either erased or at the very least changed forever.

They were only able to bring what would fit into the small apartment, and only Will's younger brother Merlin came to help. For three straight days, Will and Merl made trips back and forth, one pickup truckload at a time. They squeezed as much as they could into that tiny apartment, but whatever would not fit was simply left behind.

Merlin remembered back to the day when his older brother gave him his first car and saw that now Will needed some help, so he left him with an old Buick sedan to help them get around for the short term.

Time marched on and over the summer, Carol made life feel normal for the kids with trips to the park and visits to Grandma and Grandpa's house as Will continued to look for work. But he was clearly broken by all that had happened, and that sparkle in his eyes and energetic personality was now absent.

IT WAS LATE ON A CLEAR BUT COOL AUGUST NIGHT AS Will sat up alone. The TV was on, although he was not really watching anything. The glow from the screen added an eerie feeling to an already small, crowded, and very quiet apartment. Will was distracted and feeling more down than usual. He was doubting himself and revisiting his father's failures from the past while comparing them to his own and was beginning to question his ability to recover from this mess that he created.

Will was always an emotional man, but tonight there were no tears of either joy or sadness in his eyes, just an expressionless stare. And although it was well after midnight, he decided to quietly leave the apartment while Carol and the kids slept. He got to his car in the parking lot and quietly sat inside for several minutes, just staring off into the distance.

A tree in the vacant lot next door reminded him of the old oak tree that was so important to him and Carol when they were younger. He stared at that tree intently before he turned the key to start the car.

For reasons unknown to him, he drove back to that oak tree as if somehow drawn to it. On this clear and dark night, the only light was from his headlights as he approached. He clicked on his bright lights and came to a stop with "their tree" fully illuminated and framed in light. Will got out of the car and just stood quietly in the peaceful darkness staring at the tree.

Will turned, walked to the rear of the car, and opened the trunk. He reached in and grabbed a length of heavy rope that he had neatly coiled next to the spare tire. He walked back to the front of the car with the rope held tightly in his right hand and continued to stare at "their tree."

Memories were flooding in; he imagined himself standing under the tree with his arms wrapped tightly around Carol's waist. He heard Carol's familiar whisper of "I love you" in his ear but then realized that it was not him that he saw holding Carol at all. It was another man who held her close now. A man whom he did not recognize. Puzzled, Will looked closer and saw his two small children as they ran toward this stranger. They yelled, "Daddy, Daddy!" in excitement as they leaped into the arms of this unknown man. The vacant look on Will's face was replaced by confusion and disbelief. His right hand released the rope, which fell to the ground and impacted the dust that covered the dirt road.

In that moment, Will remembered what his father once said after he learned that a friend and neighboring farmer committed suicide during the Great Depression: "I always thought suicide was a long-term solution to a short-term problem." As Will stood there in the darkness, he had never felt more alone. A tear began to form in his right eye and rolled down his cheek as he gently began to smile.

This tear wasn't formed from sadness, self-loathing, or despair, but instead from the fond memories of all the times he and Carol shared under that tree. And the realization that if he were gone, someone else would most certainly fall in love with Carol and share his life with her. He would not allow what he had imagined in that moment to be his wife's and children's future.

The sight of that tree gave him hope for the future. Will dropped to his knees; they settled into the dust next to the rope that he no longer needed. He folded his hands, lowered his head, and prayed. He started by thanking God for the many blessings in his life, and Carol and his kids were foremost on that list. Next, he asked God to forgive him for even considering taking the life that He had so generously given him. Then he asked God to give him the strength to carry on and recited his favorite passage of Philippians 4:13. Then surprisingly, he asked God to forgive Cain and Shaw for what they did to him and all the other victims in Grayslake.

As Will looked up at the heavens, he felt a renewed sense of purpose, comfort, and peace wash over him. He wiped the tears from his eyes, looked toward the stars, and immediately recognized that God had provided this tree to him as a symbol. He thought that if this old tree could persevere against all kinds of storms, God would certainly give him the strength to do the same. Will saw that light had begun to crack through the night sky on the eastern horizon.

Dawn was breaking through the darkness, and a new day was about to begin. Will decided that this day would be a new beginning for him as well.

Will arrived home as Carol walked into the living room thinking that he had spent another night on the couch. He grabbed her around the waist, pulled her close in a tight hug, and assured her, "I love you. I've always loved you, and I will never stop loving you. God showed me tonight that He would give me the strength to carry on." Carol looked into his eyes, saw a glimpse of the Will she fell in love with, and told him, "I love you too, Wilmer Hays. I'm glad you're home. I've missed you."

Will's faith in God was strong, but his trust and faith in his fellow man had been irrecoverably shattered. So, he decided that he would be content just living an ordinary yet simple life and gave up any desire to repeat the life they left in Grayslake.

Will finally found a job as a custodian for a nearby packaging company and chose to work the midnight shift to be alone and avoid the glare and scrutiny of others. He was only earning minimum wage and had no clear plan or pathway to get them out of that small apartment.

When Will and Carol were just married, they told each other, "We don't have much, but we have each other. And that's enough." They were right back where they started, and what they said to each other back then was still true today, but now two small children were part of the equation. So, they prayed each night for God to provide some small sign that He was listening to their prayers.

CHAPTER 20

The Hero

1966

It was just after 9 a.m. on a quiet Sunday morning when the loud door buzzer, indicating someone at the lobby door, interrupted the small apartment's silence. Will pushed the intercom button and asked, "Who is it?"

A deep voice at the other end said, "Will, my name is Russell Ray. Can I please come in and talk to you for a few minutes?"

Will recognized the name as a prominent attorney in Libertyville and the founder of Mundelein Bank and Trust. As he pushed the door buzzer button for him to enter, Carol asked, "Who is that?"

Will replied, "He's an attorney in town."

Mr. Ray knocked at the door and Will invited him inside. "Good morning, Will. As mentioned, my name is Russell Ray. We haven't met before, and I do apologize for the early visit on a Sunday morning, but I wanted to try to find a time that the whole family would be home together."

"Please come in," Will invited. "This is my wife, Carol."

Carol, always the hostess, brought coffee to the very crowded and cluttered living room. Mr. Ray, a very tall and thin man, reminded Carol of Abraham Lincoln both in appearance and mannerisms, but without the beard and stovepipe hat.

Mr. Ray started the conversation. "Will, I cannot, and will not, break any attorney-client privileges, but I can say that I was asked by the Illinois state attorney general to help review everything that happened at GNB.

"It is my conclusion and belief that you did not do anything except work extremely hard in your years at GNB, and I saw plenty of evidence that supports that. And I also know that there is absolutely no evidence of you doing anything wrong there."

Mr. Ray continued, "Listen, I know how hard you worked up there, and I can't tell you how badly I feel about how you and your family were treated." Carol and Will both swallowed hard, and tears started to fill their eyes as they recognized Mr. Ray's empathy toward them. "The fact that you were basically run out of town, penniless, is unforgivable, and that entire community should be ashamed of themselves. I am very sorry that happened to you. Now there is not a lot that can be done about what happened in the past. We can't change any of that, but I do want to try to help you and your family as you move forward. If you and Carol would allow me, I would very much like to help." He went on, "I own a house here in Libertyville that I built a few years ago as a rental property. My renter has recently moved out, and the house has been empty since. It's a nice little two-story house with three bedrooms, one and a half bathrooms, a full basement, and a detached two-car garage. It is just about eighteen hundred square feet and sits on a large lot with plenty of mature trees, so you'll have plenty of room for the kids to grow and play. All the appliances are included and in good working order, so I think it could be perfect for you if you are interested."

Will wiped away a tear and said, "Mr. Ray, I… We appreciate your kindness and generosity, but I'm wondering if we can even afford the house. We are renting this small apartment now for just under $400 a month, and we can barely afford this."

Mr. Ray answered, "Will, I want to help you and Carol get back on your feet as quickly as possible. So, if you can just cover the cost of the property taxes on the house, that's all I need. And right now, that's about $225 a month." He paused. "Tell you what, before we get too far ahead of ourselves, grab the kiddos, and let's take a ride over and look at the house and see what you actually think of it." Will and Carol gathered their kids, climbed into their car, and followed Mr. Ray on the short drive over to Park Avenue near the old Libertyville Township High School.

For the first time in a long time, Will and Carol held hands. They smiled and fell in love with the house almost instantly. The exterior was clad in cream-colored stucco, green trim, and green shingles. The long gravel driveway led to a detached two-car garage that matched the house. Inside they found a beautiful large kitchen with a built-in breakfast nook that faced south and got lots of morning sun. Right off the kitchen was a large, formal dining room and an attached three-season room that also connected to the front porch. As they walked in the front door, they found a large living room with a wood-burning fireplace and built-in bookcases with glass doors on each side. Completing the first floor was a half-bath for guests and a small den.

A wide staircase with ornamental wood banisters and spindles led upstairs to a landing with large windows that provided nice views of the large, tree-lined backyard. They made the turn to the second floor where a master bedroom and two smaller bedrooms shared a full bathroom. Between the carpeting and the hardwood floors, the house was beautiful. Mr. Ray was right, it was perfect for them. It was the exact house they would have tried to find just a year earlier.

Mr. Ray told them that they could stay "as long as they like" and that he would not raise the rent unless the property taxes increased dramatically. He added that even if that did happen, they would discuss it well in advance. All Mr. Ray asked from them in return was that they maintain the home, decorate it to their taste, and treat it as if it were their own.

While Will and Carol stood quietly in what was now their new kitchen, they looked at each other, bewildered. Who was this man, and what had they done to deserve this level of kindness and generosity?

Mr. Ray walked out the back door with them, handed them a set of keys to their new home, and told them, "A moving truck will be at the apartment next Saturday morning to help you get moved. I have a friend in the moving business who owes me a big favor, so there won't be any charge for the move. We'll talk again next week to decide on when the rent will begin. Just take your time, get your family settled, and we'll figure it out as we go."

Will and Carol each grabbed one of the kids and shared a family hug right there in the driveway. With no other explanation, they were convinced that this was the sign they asked God to provide them, seeing this as evidence that God was working to help them. They cherished their time with their kids and loved being together in their new home.

CHAPTER 21

The Bank Bag

1967

It was a Friday night in early May as Will helped to get the kids to bed before he kissed Carol goodnight, walked out the back door, and found a handwritten note on his windshield.

"Meet me at Adler Park tomorrow morning after work. Come alone and don't tell anyone."

Questions raced through his mind. What did the note mean? Who wrote it? Who knew where Will lived? Why would anyone want to meet him, and so secretly?

It was an overcast morning. A light, misty rain fell as he walked to his car after work. After checking to see if any other notes had been left, he drove north along Milwaukee Avenue and headed to Adler Park, a large public park that covered close to four hundred acres along the Des Plaines River in north Libertyville. Its many wooded sections and trails provided plenty of escape routes for whoever had left the note. Will followed the road as it wound through rolling greenspaces. At 7:15 a.m. on a Saturday morning, the park seemed devoid of activity. So Will had no expectation of seeing anyone there except the person who had left the note. He drove past the swimming pool, then looked closely at the large area of picnic pavilions before turning into a parking lot that led down to an old gazebo next to the river. (A remnant of the old Adler estate…circa 1900.) He saw no cars parked, so he intended to just circle through and head back to the road. But as he started his turn, he saw someone standing in the distance. He stopped to get a better look and saw that there was definitely a person standing in the fog next to the old gazebo.

Will, nervous and more afraid than he would ever admit, nevertheless parked his car and walked down the path alone. As he got closer, he called out, "Hello?"

The man's face slowly came into view.

It was Cain.

Will was stunned and at a loss for words. He just stood there.

Cain started, "Will, I'm sorry!"

Will made the quick turn to leave.

Cain yelled out, "Will, wait. Just wait. You really do need to hear this. All of this."

Will turned back abruptly and angrily asked, "Why? Why did you do this to me?"

Cain, "Will, please listen…. I need to get this out. And you need to hear all of this from the beginning."

Will was defiant as he adjusted his weight, stood with his arms firmly crossed, and decided that he was determined to hear this.

Cain began. "Back in 1957, me and Shaw were visited at the bank by leaders of the Outfit."

Will exclaimed in sarcastic disbelief, "The mob?"

"Yes, I know it's hard to believe, but it's true. Some prosecutor named Sam Livingston was making all kinds of trouble for them in Chicago, so they needed to move cash from their downtown banks to north suburban banks like ours. And Allen and I agreed to help them."

Cain continued, "Their plan was to spread money out over existing accounts. But there was going to be so much cash coming in, we knew that we had to grow the number of accounts to do it.

"So, we knew that we had to hire someone to help us, and that's why I went to Madison. And as it turned out, we needed you." Cain continued, "But over time, they brought us so much cash that you couldn't add enough accounts to keep up with it, so I had to start writing more and more off as losses. And that showed me how I could start skimming cash that wasn't allocated to accounts. With all this cash coming in off the books, the Outfit couldn't say too much about how we were doing it because they didn't want anyone to find out what they were doing either."

Will listened as his one-time friend and mentor admitted to being a criminal and confessed to stealing money from the mob. All while thinking back to what FBI agents had told him about millions of dollars being stolen.

Will, getting increasingly agitated, cut Cain off. "So you decided to steal millions of dollars from the mob, and that wasn't enough for you? You needed to steal $35,000 from me and ruin my life in the process?"

Cain replied, "I am sorry about that, Will. I really am. But please let me explain why I did it. Allen and I knew that someone was going to find out what we were doing sooner or later. If the feds found out, we would spend the rest of our lives in prison. And if the Outfit found out, they would have killed all of us without even thinking twice about it. So, when we found out the feds were getting close, we took as much as we could and ran.

"Will, we are both in our sixties now, and we don't have kids and families. We can stay hidden for the rest of our lives. But you are a young man, and you have a family with little kids." He held his hand flat at his thigh to indicate their stature. "You are, and always will be, a good man and a great friend, and we just couldn't allow you to get dragged into this. The only way I could think to keep you out of all this was to make you a victim as well. I had to, or the feds and mob would have thought you were in on it with us. Leaving you bankrupt was not an easy decision for me, but it was the only way I could keep you and your family clean and safe. If it wasn't completely obvious to everyone, the FBI would have charged you as an accomplice, and the Outfit would have had you, Carol, and probably the kids all killed. I just couldn't let that happen."

Will clenched his fists inside his pockets, took a deep breath, and angrily responded, "What about all the money you stole from the people that I brought to the bank? They trusted me."

Cain stood quietly and expressionless. He just nodded in agreement and mumbled, "That's true" under his breath.

Will threw his hands up in the air. "So why now? Why tell me all of this now?"

"Because this is the last time you will ever see me. Shaw is already gone forever."

"You could have just called me on the phone. Why risk meeting me like this?"

Cain answered, "Because I needed you to know the truth, and I needed you to hear it from me, in person. And I also needed to give you this before I disappear." Cain gave Will the blue canvas bank bag he'd been holding all this time and said, "Will, I am truly sorry for what I did, but I just couldn't think of any other way to keep you out of this. I hope someday you'll be able to forgive me."

Will watched as Cain walked away into the woods along the river's edge and slowly disappeared into the fog. He then looked in all directions to see if anyone else was watching him before he made the walk back to his car. He was nervous and thought to himself that the bag Cain gave him was quite heavy. Although curious about its contents, he decided to drive home before he looked inside.

Will checked his mirrors frequently and made several random turns along the route home to ensure he was not followed. Once home, he entered through the back door. It was still early on a Saturday morning. With the house quiet, he suspected that Carol and the kids were still asleep.

Will went straight down to the basement and carefully made his way through the darkness to his workbench in the back corner. He set the bag down and reached up to flip on the overhead work light before opening the bag's drawstrings to look inside. He pulled out a roll of coins and held it to the light. The paper roll read, "$10 Quarters." He pulled out the next roll—again, "$10 Quarters." He stacked roll after roll and came to a final tally of 184 rolls.

Will thought to himself that this just added insult to injury. Still angered by what Cain had confessed to him, he could not understand why Cain would insist on leaving this with him. Why would he risk meeting over $1,840 worth of quarters?

Will sat for several minutes as he reflected on everything Cain had told him. With all the rolls now out of the bag, he reached down to the bottom and felt around to see if there was anything else inside. He found a small note card and held it to the light. The handwritten message from Cain read, "Your money back from your investment." He rested his head on his hand and looked back at the stack of rolls. He stared at them as he thought, then picked up one of the rolls to examine it more closely.

He looked at it from each end and then started to tear the paper open. Inside, he found that a quarter had been placed inside each end of the roll that allowed them to be visible through the opening at each end.

But between each quarter were $5 gold Indian Head coins. Will knew such coins had only been minted between 1910 and 1929, making these coins increasingly rare and high in value. He grabbed his scale from the shelf below his bench and weighed each roll. All had the same weight.

Will concluded that Cain had returned his $35,000 investment in $5 gold coins. That would mean a total of seven thousand gold Indian Head coins had to be hidden inside these rolls. He thought about what Cain had said earlier and decided that no one could know about these coins. Will removed the screws from the pegboard off the wall behind his workbench and began to neatly stack each roll in the wall for safekeeping.

Will spent a lot of time sitting by that workbench, thinking back to his youth and early days with Carol. He reflected on what his life was like before, during, and now after Grayslake. He had dreamed of being successful and providing his family with opportunities that he did not have. These coins certainly meant that his children, grandchildren, and perhaps even great-grandchildren would have the opportunities he worked so hard to achieve.

He had survived the Great Depression and a difficult childhood, learning firsthand what life was like without the luxuries and trappings of modern life.

Will refused to get caught up in the potential value of these coins. He could provide a happy and fruitful life for himself and his family without that money. He decided to take the lessons learned in Grayslake to heart. Houses, cars, and perhaps most importantly now, money, had absolutely nothing to do with success or happiness.

A COUPLE OF MONTHS LATER, WILL LEFT WORK AT HIS usual time, got in his car, and turned on the engine. As he turned on the headlights, he was startled to see a large man standing in front of his car. It was Baker, though Will did not recognize him. Will hastily locked his door as the seemingly unknown man approached, causing Will to immediately think back to everything Cain had told him. Only someone who was going to be trouble would surely be standing alone in the darkness waiting for him. Will also knew that if he could see one man in front of him, there was probably more that he couldn't see behind him.

Baker rapped his knuckles on his window and said, "Will, I'm not here to hurt you. I just need to talk to you."

Will cracked his window open an inch and asked, "What do you want?"

Baker said, "If I were here to kill you, you'd be dead already. I need you to get out of the car for a minute and talk to me."

Will was terrified but thought that in some weird way what the man said made sense, so he cracked the door open and reluctantly got out. Will looked up at Baker's imposing figure as Baker said, "I'm looking for Gordon Cain. When was the last time you saw him?"

Will replied, "The day before he ruined my life."

"Do you have any idea where he is?"

Will answered, "I have no idea…nor do I care."

"You don't seem to be too angry over someone that ruined your life."

Will answered, "I was angry. I am angry, but I can't live every day of my life angry about something that I can't change. And honestly, I'm more afraid of you right now than I ever was angry with Cain."

Baker replied, "Relax, I'm not here to hurt you. I just need your help."

"I haven't seen him since he took our money."

Baker asked, "Our money? What do you mean?"

"I'm assuming he took your money too. Isn't that why you are looking for him? The FBI agents at the bank asked me about someone named Lennox. Is that you?"

Baker answered, "No, but I work for him. Cain stole his money just like he stole yours. Just a lot more of it."

"Well, Cain didn't actually steal my money. I was stupid and walked into his office and handed him a check."

Baker replied, "My boss trusted him with his money too, and I would never call him stupid. He just trusted the wrong person, the same as you."

"So now what? I don't know where Cain is. And I really don't care."

"Go to work and forget you ever saw me," said Baker. "And stay away from Cain because if I ever find out that he contacted you, or that there is even a hint of you having any of our money, then next time you and I will have a very different conversation."

That surprise visit was enough to convince Will that everything Cain told him was probably true and that he would always need to think about who might be watching him and his family.

From that moment on, Will went out of his way to avoid drawing any attention to himself and focused on what truly mattered to him: his everlasting love for and devotion to his wife and his children. Will and Carol stayed in the house on Park Avenue and raised their two children there. Both kids were happy, healthy, and well-adjusted. They both graduated high school, and his daughter went on to be the first in the family to attend and graduate from college. She attended law school and built a very successful career, becoming highly respected in her field, while his son worked in law enforcement and enjoyed a distinguished career as a police officer. You may have already guessed that son is me, Jeffrey Hays.

CHAPTER 22

The Treasure

PRESENT DAY

I think about my parents frequently and I know they were very proud of the lives their children built for themselves and even more importantly, the people they became. Mom and Dad struggled for many years but I think they would say that they lived full and happy lives together, and as they got older, they settled comfortably into the roles of Grandma and Grandpa to my kids.

My sister and I, like most children, watched as our parents aged and their health declined. With them no longer able to live safely in their home on their own, we had to make the extremely difficult decision to move them out of their house and into an assisted living community.

As I undertook the enormous task of cleaning out our parents' home, I found that my dad had, in fact, kept everything. And I mean everything. I found old bicycles, old baseball uniforms, trading cards, report cards, and nearly every toy from our youth. As unbelievable as it may seem, I even found every check my dad had ever written and every tax form he ever filed.

So, it is no exaggeration for me to say he kept everything. Every nook and cranny of the basement and the attic was like a time capsule preserved just for me and my sister. I viewed all of them as special gifts from my dad. But ultimately, there was no Picasso hidden in the attic. Just plenty of evidence of a happy, yet frugal, life.

All the things important and valuable to Mom and Dad were kept inside a safe in a locked room in the basement. My dad had frequently shared with me that when the time came to open the safe, I would find life insurance policies, wills, passports, and the adoption paperwork for both me and my sister.

Included in this paperwork was a plain white envelope that had "Treasure Map" written in Dad's handwriting. As I opened this envelope, I could not help but smile in anticipation of what Dad might describe as "treasure." I could not wait to get started.

I followed the hand-drawn map, a process that, with the basement now almost emptied, did not take nearly as long as I'm sure Dad anticipated. As I reached the "X" on the map, I found myself standing in front of Dad's workbench. Throughout my life, I had garnered plenty of experience with that bench and knew that everything had its place and that all his tools were to be replaced properly when the job was finished. The instructions said to look behind Grandpa's saw. I knew immediately that he meant the handsaw given to him by his father in his first toolbox. Dad never used this saw. It just hung proudly on display on a hook on the pegboard above his bench. I knew how important that saw was to him. I think it not only reminded him of his father, but he also viewed the saw as a gesture from his dad that almost became like an apology for a lifetime of distance between them.

And for years it served as a visual reminder of Dad's wish and desire to forgive his father. I was told to never touch it, let alone use it. So, it made perfect sense to me that Dad would keep his "treasure" near this saw. I moved the saw to the side and did not see anything on the pegboard behind it but dust and cobwebs. I grabbed the nearby flashlight and used it to study the pegboard more closely; through the peg openings, I noticed something behind the board, within the wall.

Using a screwdriver, I removed the screws on each corner, and then as I removed the board, I saw what to me looked like about one hundred rolls of quarters stacked neatly within the wall. I smiled and chuckled to myself at the thought of this being Dad's "treasure." I had heard stories about his old banking days and knew of his small collection of silver dollars but thought it funny that he had stuffed all these quarters into the wall for me to find this way. In total, I found 182 rolls of quarters.

When I saw him the next day on my daily visit and told him, "Hey, Dad, I found your treasure. Very funny," he stood abruptly from his chair and said, "Let's take a walk." He invited me down the hallway with him and said he needed to talk to me away from Mom so she wouldn't overhear. We walked to the end of the hallway near the elevators and sat on a couple of the large comfortable chairs they kept there. And for the next couple of hours, Dad relived and shared his entire story with me.

He started by saying, "It turns out that this whole thing started because of some guy named 'Sam Livingston' who got himself elected as a prosecutor in Cook County. Cain told me that his election was the one thing that caused all of this to happen."

From there Dad told me how he met Cain in Madison and then met Shaw, and everything that unfolded in Grayslake. He told me the story of how he got the rolls of quarters from Cain in 1967 and discovered the gold coins hidden inside each roll. Dad went on to say that he took one of the coins to a coin shop in Waukegan to have it appraised and that each coin was valued at about $35, making the coins' total value in 1968 about $245,000.

Between 1968 and today, Dad told me that he had only sold off a couple of rolls of coins and that he would just sell a few coins at a time when he was short on money. And that "just to be safe" he had driven to a different coin shop each time. He said that even today it was still important to be careful and think about what we were doing with the coins. He felt that this was a "treasure" for the family now and that we should keep it secret and not draw attention to ourselves.

I asked, "Why did Cain give you all of this in gold coins?"

Dad said, "Cain knew I wouldn't take any money from him. But by giving me these $5 coins, he knew I would see it as an actual repayment rather than just a gift or bribe to ease his guilt. He also knew that the gold over time would be my 'return on the investment,' and the longer I held onto them, the more they would be worth. And he was right," Dad said with a big grin. "In today's gold market, the coins are worth about 3 million dollars."

When I heard that, I sat thoroughly astonished and dumbfounded. Profanity was never allowed in my parents' house, and so I had trained myself to refrain from using any in front of them, but I just couldn't help the words from racing out of my mouth: "Are you fucking kidding me?"

Dad shrugged and offered a sheepish grin as if to say, "Can you believe it?"

I asked, "After all this time, is there any way, or would it even be possible, that anyone would come looking for this money?"

Dad answered, "I don't know. I guess it's possible."

I felt like I was in shock, so I took a couple of deep breaths as I thought about what to say next. I leaned forward in my chair and asked, "Three million dollars? You kept 3 million dollars hidden in the basement all these years?" I sat there thinking about those questions for what felt like ten minutes before I said, "Dad, what is the point of having all this money if you can't do anything with it? Somehow, you've managed to keep it secret all these years. And now you are telling me that if you did decide to spend some, you would need to look over your shoulder for the rest of your life? That just seems pointless to me."

Dad said that he had spent countless hours sitting at his workbench alone in the quiet, thinking about that very thing. He never came up with a workable solution, so he just continued to keep them hidden. He was always reluctant to let go of the money and kept circling back to the idea that these coins were family money and should become an inheritance for me and my sister.

I said, "Dad, these men stole everything from you in 1965, and you were never truly repaid. Somehow you have managed to live your life without this money and were able to overcome that level of loss. You made it through without it, so do you really think it's worth all the problems or risk they could create now?"

Dad and I talked almost exclusively about this over the next few days, and we discussed several ideas of what we could do with these coins. One idea was to donate the money to charities. We talked about different organizations that could benefit from it and how we could do something for them while still avoiding any paper trail or unwanted attention on us.

We decided that the best thing we could do was donate what was left, and the sheer number of lives that could benefit from this made our decision that much easier.

I told Dad that I had heard a news story that every year, The Salvation Army finds several rare gold coins in their donation kettles from random, anonymous donors. I said that I thought that idea could work for us and that The Salvation Army probably had some kind of mechanism or system in place to watch for these gold coins. Our hope was that this organization would recognize that these coins had a much higher value than just what was stamped on them at the mint.

The decision was made, and that following December, I picked up Dad early on a Saturday morning, and we went for a ride to enact our plan. We set out that day to find as many Salvation Army donation kettles as we could, with each kettle getting a handful of coins. As I walked to that first kettle and heard the bell ringing louder and louder as I approached, I remember having the distinct feeling of second-guessing myself.

What were we doing? Were we crazy? This was more money than I would ever see in my lifetime, and we were giving it all away? I walked back to the car and asked Dad, "Are we doing the right thing?"

Dad said, "In the letter to the Corinthians we are told that God loves a cheerful giver. Those that sow sparingly will also reap sparingly, and to those who sow generously will also reap generously." He smiled at me and simply said, "There are people that need this money more than we do. We have each other, and that's always been enough for me."

I turned to head back to that first kettle and thought to myself that I knew when I accepted the job as a police officer that I was never going to be a millionaire. And I also knew that Dad grew up without money and that he never really had any money for most of his adult life either.

That is when I realized, and quickly came to terms with, the fact that our lives today were no different than when I discovered this "treasure" hidden in the wall. So, it did not take long for me to come to terms with the fact that neither of us was going to miss money that we really never had anyway.

That's when I recognized the special feeling of helping so many people who needed it so much more than us. A sense of pride washed over me as those first few coins slid into the kettle. And when I got back to the car, the look on Dad's face confirmed that he shared in that joyous feeling.

We drove together all day throughout Libertyville and Mundelein as I made countless stops, running a handful of coins at a time to each of the kettles until only about ten coins remained. Just enough for one last stop. I asked Dad, "Should we make our last stop in Grayslake?"

Dad replied, "That's a good idea. Let's do that."

I made the short drive into Grayslake, and we drove right into downtown on Center Street as Dad called out a couple of the business names that he still recognized from all those years ago. As we approached the GNB building, wouldn't you know it—there was a Salvation Army volunteer stationed right at the front door.

This was perfect, so I pulled up along the curb, parked the car, and walked around to open the door to help Dad out. I took him by the arm, and we walked together, arm in arm, to that final kettle. I will always remember the sound of those coins as they left Dad's hand and hit that metal lid before sliding into the kettle below, one after another

The Treasure

until the last coin disappeared as Dad uttered, "Well, that's it." That was immediately followed by a "Merry Christmas" from the woman seated on the stool and ringing the bell. And just like that it was all gone. The last connection and memory of what happened in Grayslake was finally, and thankfully, gone forever. I held Dad's arm as we walked back to the car. He stopped suddenly to look at me and said, "I held onto those coins for a long time." As he opened his hand to show me that he had kept one, he said, "I think I need to hold onto this one for a little while longer, if that's okay with you?"

My only response was to smile and say, "Dad, you've kept everything else in your life. I wouldn't expect anything less from you at this point." Dad looked up at me and smiled as we stood in the shadow of the building that started all this. And on that cold day, all I could do was wrap my arms around him and hug him tight. I felt his warm breath on my neck as he whispered in my ear, "I love you, Jeffer." I simply whispered back, "I love you too, Dad."

As odd as it may seem, that is one of my favorite and lasting memories of my dad.

Years later when Dad died, I found that very same coin sealed in a plain white envelope locked securely in his safe; on the envelope, he had written, "Jeffer's Treasure." And again, Dad was right. That coin reminds me of how important my memories of that day are to me. That treasure, I'll keep with me for the rest of my life.

Epilogue

It was 7:29 a.m. on what turned out to be an overcast and rainy Monday morning in August. What would have been just another ordinary, perhaps even forgettable, day was forever changed when my phone rang, awakening me from a sound sleep. I reached for it on my nightstand and saw that it was my sister calling. We had both been caring for our elderly parents for several years, but their health had steadily declined over the last few days and weeks. So, a call this early in the morning most certainly meant that bad news was headed in my direction. I sat up in bed, swung my legs over the side, and rested my feet on the side rails as I said, "Hi, Sara." I could hear the tears in her voice and lump in her throat as she prepared herself to completely devastate her brother. Then she bravely said the three words that I had grown to fear most. "Dad is dead." I dropped the phone on the floor, and with my elbows resting on my knees, I put my head in my hands, sat there on the edge of the bed, and sobbed.

Something deep inside me forever changed that day. It was more than just having my heart broken. That happens to everybody who loses someone they love, but for me, every fiber of my being and soul now seemed torn and raw. I felt different. I was different, and now everything in my life was different. Because the most important and loved man in my life was gone forever. I struggled with that loss then, and I still do today.

I remember the first Sunday morning after Dad's funeral. I set my alarm to get up early so I would have plenty of time to shower and shave before I put on my best suit and leather wingtip shoes and tied the perfect Windsor knot.

Dad always wore a suit or sport coat to church, but either way he always looked his best, and I wanted to do the same for him. So I finished getting dressed, checked myself in the mirror, and off I went to the 8 a.m. service at the very same church where I said goodbye to him at his funeral just a few days earlier.

I thought that by going to the church that he loved and wearing what he typically wore to church, it would somehow make me feel close to him again. Instead, I sat alone in the church pew and felt like a stranger sitting in someone else's living room. Instead of feeling closer to him, I felt like he was even further away. After the service, I was not sure what to do next or how to deal with what I was feeling, so I decided to make the short drive over to the cemetery where he was laid to rest. I stood at the foot of his freshly covered grave, the loose dirt still piled up with fresh flowers from the funeral arranged neatly on top. It was there that I told Dad how much I loved and missed him and how grateful I was for everything that he had done for me.

I did not say these things because I felt regret or because he had not heard me say them before. It was quite the opposite. I don't ever remember a time when my dad and I were in the same room when we didn't hug and say that we loved each other.

He was a great role model for me and gave me the greatest gift of all by teaching me how to be a good father to my children. He knew that I loved him every day of my life as I knew that he loved me every day of his. Neither one of us had regrets about any of that. Dad and I did not share a single strand of DNA, but there was never any question or doubt that he was my father.

He was not my friend. And I was not his. I was the son. He was the father. And he was everything to me, so now I stand alone at his gravesite every Sunday morning, rain or shine, to say just that.

And I've been doing this every week since he died. It's gotten to the point that I'm beginning to think there might be something wrong with me. I find myself looking around the cemetery only to find that I am the only one here. In a cemetery with hundreds, if not thousands, of headstones, I am alone. All these people buried here were loved by their families as much as I loved my dad. And are most certainly missed by their families as much as I miss him. But here I stand alone. So why am I having so much difficulty letting go of my dad? When it appears to me that everyone else manages to move on more quickly?

Then one day, a sobering realization came to me. He was my example, my teacher. I have learned everything I know from him. And he never let anything go. Starting with the teasing he got from his older brother growing up. I'm sure he carried that with him most of his life. He married his one true love and soulmate, and I'm certain he would have never let her go even if he had the chance to. He bought his first, and only, new car in 1957 but kept the old 1946 Fleetline instead of trading it in. And ultimately, I don't think he ever let go of what happened in Grayslake. I think that weighed on him every day of his life.

As I spend more time thinking about that these days, I find myself more and more interested in the part of Dad's life that either I was not present for or was too young to remember. And although he was open and shared many details of his life with me, I have discovered plenty of things that I did not know about him. And still don't.

I think that children see their parents in a variety of lights, but none truly have the full measure of reality. I found that my perception of my father became very different than the reality, and it was only as I grew older and began leading an adult life that I was able to dissect just who these people were who raised me. I was too young to remember anything about our life in Grayslake. As I grew older, I was blinded by the irresponsibilities of youth and frankly, just so selfish and preoccupied with what was going on with me and in my life that I never clearly saw how much my parents struggled with all of this. I was raised by this man and lived with him for my first twenty years, but paid no attention to anything he was going through. And now, I am truly embarrassed and ashamed to admit that.

I realized much too late how my father and I never talked in any meaningful detail about what our life had been like in Grayslake, and now more importantly to me, why we left. I would hear the occasional anecdote about his work in banking, but he did not share many details, and I definitely don't remember hearing any names associated with his time there.

As I grew more interested in visiting that time in his life, I was fortunate in that my father kept everything from his past. I found boxes and boxes of old photographs, newspaper clippings, and plenty of mementos of Mom and Dad's life together. I have spent countless hours going through each of these boxes, which were full of photos of my parents as young kids growing up in the 1930s and 1940s. My mother in Oglesby and Lasalle, and my father on several farms throughout western Illinois.

I found the records of my father's time in the Marine Corps, including his time at Camp Pendleton, and pictures of Mom and Dad's first rental house together in Oceanside, CA. I found a photo of Dad's first car, the 1946 Chevrolet Fleetline (the one that I can't seem to quit talking about) as he drove down the gravel road at the farm in LaSalle, and the very same car that Mom and Dad drove cross country after their wedding.

I found high school yearbooks from LaSalle Peru High School that show Dad as a senior and Mom as a junior. They included photos of Mom performing on stage in both theater and chorus productions. I found wedding photos and a picture that Dad took of Mom picnicking on a blanket under "their tree."

I found Dad's banking certificates from the American Institute of Banking, Southern Illinois University, and the Graduate School of Banking at the University of Wisconsin-Madison. I even found a class photo from Madison that showed all 140 students from the class he attended there with Dad standing proudly right in the center. I stumbled across the silver tie clip that Mom had engraved for Dad on his first day of work at GNB, along with many pictures of the Grayslake house on Harvey Avenue at various stages of construction, some of which even show the 1957 Larkspur-blue Chevy Bel Air parked out front.

I located the bill of sale for the 1962 Cadillac tucked in with a picture taken on the day Dad bought it. And many newspaper clippings of him being elected vice president of the local chapter of the Jaycees and president of the Grayslake Chamber of Commerce. There was also a photo of Mom and Dad carrying me and my sister as they led the Fourth of July parade. And surprisingly enough, I even found a picture of Mom and Dad being crowned king and queen of Judy Lee Jewels.

In the end, I found memories and evidence of every single part of their lives together.

What I did not find in any of these boxes were any pictures of Gordon Cain. I did not find any of Allen and Delores Shaw either.

The reason for this is simply because they do not exist. Lennox, Garrett, Barnes, Baker, Livingston, and La Monica do not exist either. They were all created by me to offer an explanation and solution to what has become a very difficult and complex question for me.

What happened in Grayslake?

Dad as a young man was clearly ambitious, and there is plenty of evidence of that and his desire for success. He decided at a very early age that he wanted, even craved, success. And the reality is that by almost every account, plenty of evidence supports him achieving it. But after Grayslake, with everything gone, his worst fear was that he would forever be remembered as a failure. He most certainly was not.

As a child and an adolescent, Dad had nothing. Life on the farm was difficult for him, with early morning chores followed by school and then back home for more chores. All while being tormented by an arrogant and entitled older brother and desperately trying to please an emotionally distant father.

At eighteen years of age, he enlisted in the Marine Corps to escape a life of struggle on the farm that he knew he did not want.

At twenty years, he married the love of his life and the inspiration to become his best self.

At twenty-two, he was honorably discharged from the Marine Corps and began the five-year process of completing not one but three separate continuing education programs from highly regarded institutions.

At twenty-eight, he left his job at Ottawa National Bank and used the level of education and experience he had achieved there to land a great new job at Grayslake National Bank. That same year he purchased his very first new car and started construction on a new home. The first and only home he would ever own.

At thirty years, he found himself well-liked and respected enough in the Grayslake community to be elected Chamber of Commerce secretary and then Chamber of Commerce president just a couple of years later, becoming one of the youngest presidents the Grayslake Chamber ever had.

At thirty-one, he adopted his first child, a son.

At thirty-three, he adopted his second child, a daughter and my sister.

At thirty-six, he and his wife decided to incorporate and began building a very successful second business.

At thirty-seven, he had made it. By most standards, he was living the American dream with a beautiful and loving wife, two healthy and happy kids, a great job, a home of his own, friends, cars, and money. He was a respected part of the business community and had established roots living within that same community.

And then at thirty-eight, in what seemed like just a blink of an eye, it was all gone. In a matter of weeks, everything changed. The job, the house, the cars, the friends… Everything. Mom and Dad fled Grayslake and moved to a different town with two small children in tow and into a small two-bedroom apartment.

Epilogue

So, again, I needed to ask, what caused this divergence?

For as hard as I tried to answer that question, I simply could not figure it out. And now with both of my parents gone, along with any others who could have added insight to this mystery, I came to the grim realization that I may never know exactly what happened to them.

It was then that I began writing the story of their lives together and began the process of creating Cain.

I needed to create a villain to fit into my theory that someone had caused Dad to lose everything in Grayslake. I could not imagine any scenario where he would just walk away from everything he worked so hard to build. My only solution was that someone must have taken it from him.

What I do know is that Dad did not do anything wrong or illegal at the bank that would have gotten him fired or forced him to leave. Mr. Ray (who is very much a real person) was a very well-respected attorney and the primary founder of two banks in the neighboring town of Mundelein, IL. He would not have helped my parents if he had any suspicion that Dad did something wrong in Grayslake. Of that, I am supremely confident.

Mr. Russell Ray is a true hero in this story, and without his courage, compassion, kindness, and humanity, along with his selfless willingness to help my parents in their darkest hour, I'm certain this story, and our lives, would have had a much different ending. My most heartfelt thanks go out to him.

So, I am left reluctantly with this thought. Could it be possible that Dad suffered some kind of mental breakdown or perhaps even from some level of long-term mental illness?

Is it possible that he could have put so much pressure on himself to be successful that the stress of the long hours at the bank, his family, the jewelry business, or a combination of all those, caused him to have a break or a disconnect?

I think that there is some evidence to support that possibility. After he made the move to Libertyville, most of the world saw him differently. I think they saw a broken man ready to be discarded, and I think that maybe even he recognized that he was broken. My sister and I found out many years later that our mother really did take over the responsibilities of our daily lives after Grayslake. She worked two jobs and still made time to manage our schedules, handle the money, pay the bills, keep the family fed and healthy, stay on top of our schoolwork and activities, and manage every detail of our lives. For as much as Dad wanted to believe he was "the man of the house," it truly was Mom who kept everything going.

My dad's significant contribution was that my sister and I were raised by a loving, warm, caring, compassionate, inclusive, and encouraging father completely focused on family first.

If it is true that he was broken, then I for one think he was better broken.

He was always home and always had time for me. Whether he was coaching me in Little League baseball or teaching me to push a mower or how to properly shovel snow. Getting me to church or insisting on my help in the garden. He taught me the value of hard work and that nothing worthwhile was ever going to come easily or just be handed to you. Every minute of time I had with him was valuable to both of us. He was always there and available for me, and I'm not sure I would have gotten any of that from who he was becoming in Grayslake.

I have spent a lot of time thinking about why we left Grayslake, but I suspect all our lives would have been much different, and probably worse, if all this hadn't happened and we had stayed there.

People who are close to me often ask questions upon learning that I am writing this. They want to know whether I learned anything about my dad that I did not know before or if my opinion of him has changed in any way. I find myself reflecting on those questions separately and have found that my answer to the first is for me a bit more complex than the second. I tried to view my dad in the full light of day and tried my best to not be overly critical or judgmental while still making every effort to be as honest as I could. What I did learn was that Dad was very much a human being and much less a superhero. He was flawed and certainly had deep-seated insecurities, self-doubt, and issues with trusting others. I also think it is possible that he suffered from some levels of depression and may have had some self-destructive tendencies. His childhood ambitions certainly contributed to his vanity and unbridled desire for acceptance from others. At times he would be passive-aggressive, manipulative, temperamental, and stubborn. But what I found, which was an integral part of this exercise, was that to get the full picture of who a human being is, you cannot only focus on their negative traits. You need to be thorough and include evidence of character, caring, integrity, honesty, and most importantly love.

For me the second question is much easier to answer. And that answer is an emphatic no, my opinion of my father is no different today than it ever was. He was perfect in every way.

I prefer to, and always will, see him just as he was. No matter what happened in Grayslake, my father was a strong man with strong convictions and an unwavering faith in

God. He had a selfless dedication to family, and I am eternally grateful for the life he provided me.

Whatever it was that made him abandon the life he worked so hard to build in Grayslake, it might have been easier for him to give up or quit, but to his credit, he never did, and I am proud of him in every way for that. After Grayslake, he lived the remainder of his life demonstrating words like integrity, character, and honesty. He set a great example for me by telling the truth, working hard, and caring about his neighbors. I never witnessed any bravado from him. He was never one to beat his chest or demand the spotlight.

He was the salt of the earth and seemed content in the notion that he was not exceptional. He did not allow himself to be defined by what others thought of or said about him. And until now, Wilmer Hays was a man very few people outside of Grayslake or Libertyville even knew. I feel confident now saying that he may have been one of the most sincere and genuine men you never met. It brought him joy meeting and talking to new people, and he didn't draw conclusions about someone's character or worth based on the color of their skin, what they did for a living, what their address was, or who they voted for in the last election. I think the world could use more people like that these days.

So, through all this I have been waiting patiently for the pain of him leaving me to ease, and I realize now, that will never happen. I will miss him every day for the remainder of my life. And in a strange way that makes me smile, because I know this pain I feel helps to keep him with me.

My one regret from the onset was that my dad did not get to hear me say, "I love you" that one last time. But I can't help but think that perhaps because of that, I have found other ways to say it each day since. So, with that I will leave you with this sentiment. I make it a point to say these four words out loud every day. And if at any point you find yourself thinking about your dad as you read this, feel free to say them with me.

I love you, Dad.

Dad driving his first car. The 1946 Chevrolet Fleetline.

Acknowledgments

I wish to extend my heartfelt gratitude to Patricia Marshall and my entire publishing team at Luminare Press. With special thanks to my managing editor, Sallie Vandagrift, my copy editor, Andrea Vanryken, and my designer, Kristen Brack. Your expertise, guidance, and professionalism are invaluable and resulted in making this project the very best possible version of itself. I am very proud to have all of you associated with this book.

About the Author

J.P. HAYS is the Chicago-born author who, following the loss of his father, began writing as an exercise to work through his grief while also hoping to gain some insight into an important question raised after his father's death. What his sister initially called "a love letter to Dad" has been adapted by J.P. into the surprising story of *Creating Cain*, based on the true story of his father's life from 1957 to 1966.

J.P. completed many years in law enforcement as a police officer and is now retired, choosing to leave the cold and snow behind to enjoy life in the Smoky Mountains of Southeastern Tennessee. Today, he still applies lessons learned from his father and continues to be dedicated to the importance of family. He is a supportive and loving husband and father to his children and is now an adoring grandfather to three beautiful granddaughters. And who knows? Maybe one of them will be inspired to write a book about him someday.

www.ingramcontent.com/pod-product-compliance
Lightning Source LLC
LaVergne TN
LVHW041806060526
838201LV00046B/1148